THE TRULY HAPPY YOU

A SIMPLE GUIDE TO REIGNITING YOUR INNER SPARK

JESSICA S. ABELE

Neelam,
May you keep getting
to know yourself better —
and keep loving
what you discover!
Best,
Jessica

The Truly Happy You - A Simple Guide to Reigniting Your Inner Spark

eBook ISBN: 978-0-692-98926-5

Print ISBN: 978-0-692-05058-3

Edited by: Andrea Robinson

Cover design: Gustavo Villareal

DEDICATION

To Johnathan
You spent your life searching for your true happiness. I wish
you could be here to read my book, because maybe it would
have helped you realize...*your spark was always there.*

1

"Those who have not found their true wealth, which is the radiant joy of Being and the deep, unshakable peace that comes with it, are beggars, even if they have great material wealth. They are looking outside for scraps of pleasure or fulfillment, for validation, security, or love, while they have a treasure within that not only includes all those things but is infinitely greater than anything the world can offer." —Eckhart Tolle, *The Power of Now: A Guide to Spiritual Enlightenment*

THE TRULY HAPPY YOU

A re you happy? I mean, truly happy?

Do you feel like you should answer "yes" to this question because that's what you think people want to hear, even while deep down inside you may be screaming "no"? Do you experience guilt or sadness as you contemplate why you don't feel happy? Do you have the sensation of being lost or that something is missing from your life? Do you feel like you are playing a game of charades, masquerading happiness so that no one sees your confusion and self-doubt? Or do you simply want to breathe a little easier, smile a little bigger and enjoy your life without complexities?

I know feelings like this all too well. It wasn't that long ago that I felt lost, sad and completely hollow inside. My whole being was pleading for help, yet I was unable to hear my own cries; I was keeping up a charade, too, striving to fit into that mold of living the "perfect life." While I tried to paint a pretty picture for others to see, I made sure it never told my whole story.

I tried to be the perfect friend, quick to latch onto anyone who hinted at a possible friendship, even if we only shared one common interest. Then I'd follow them around like a puppy dog trying to make them feel as important as I was hoping they'd make me feel—as if their approval would make me feel more complete.

I tried to be the perfect wife, painting a marriage masterpiece by never letting other people witness my husband and me having even a simple disagreement. I wanted them to see a happy, loving, perfect-for-each-other couple. I also expected my husband to know what my painting looked like and how to properly conform himself to fit into it.

I even tried to be the perfect mother, one who never had to reprimand her children in public because they always acted calm and respectful. I expected my children to fit into precise little molds, which often made it difficult for me to just let them be kids.

I had become quite the artist, mastering a "perfect portrait" for every occasion. Until, one day, I realized how exhausted I was. I'd been so busy painting a perfect life, when was I actually living it?

If you are anything like I was, you are feeling rather low right now. You are having a hard time shaking off persistent feelings of emptiness and sadness. You feel angry, depressed or annoyed on a regular basis, and you can't figure out why. You tend to focus so much of your energy on how you think you should think, feel or act throughout the day that you are unable to just *be* yourself. You may also find it difficult to truly love others and have honest, meaningful relationships. I bet these things leave you feeling lonely or scared that you may never be able to truly give love or feel loved by others. And maybe, though you are scared to admit it, you have allowed thoughts of self-harm to creep in. You feel like you are on a downward spiral into a dark abyss, and you lack the energy and motivation to try to stop the free fall. You're wondering why no one seems to see or understand your struggles, and you wonder if it's even possible to feel better than this.

If you can relate to any of these things, and find that they are interfering with the ability to truly enjoy your life, then I have some good news. I wrote this book for you. It's for anyone struggling with tough emotions, and anyone who wants to feel more in tune with their true self. It's important to know that you are not destined for a life of unhappiness. I hope this book can be the catalyst you need to realize that. So please don't give up, as we are just getting started.

This story begins with my search for what was really true. A search for the real me, and through that search, real joy. It's probably similar to the one that led you here, as—let's be honest—if you are reading a book that can be located by searching keywords such as "depression," "happiness," "self-help," or "motivation," it's safe to say you're not feeling as happy as you'd like. And if you are anything like I was, you're also searching for truth and hope. You're searching for something that speaks to you, something that will help you make sense of the emotional storms you're experiencing, and something that will act as a compass to help navigate through your darkness. You're hoping to discover a spark deep in the core of your being that will illuminate your true self. And with that spark's discovery, you're hoping to feel a sense of relief, because maybe, just maybe, there is a chance for a truly happy you.

Within this book, you'll find practical, engaging and, above all, easy techniques and exercises that you can implement in your daily life, starting right now. Both realistic and rewarding, they are simple ways to help you achieve a happier and more centered life.

During the course of this book's journey, I hope to help you reawaken your inner joy by:

- Reaffirming that you are not alone in your struggles.
- Assuring that healing and happiness are possible.
- Creating a profound sense of clarity and peace within you.
- Showing you how to make powerful and positive changes within you and the world around you.
- Teaching you to enjoy the present moment without worries.
- Guiding you to discover how developing habits of self-love and gratitude can lead to enormous personal, spiritual and emotional growth.
- Sparking a transformation, within your mind and body, yes, but also in how you perceive your surroundings.

Sounds great, doesn't it? Maybe a little too great?

Let's back up for a minute.

2

"The most beautiful people we have known are those who have known defeat, known struggle, known loss and have found their way out of its depths. These persons have an appreciation, a sensitivity, and an understanding of life that fills them with compassion, gentleness, and a deep, loving concern. Beautiful people do not just happen." —Elisabeth Kubler-Ross, *Death: The Final Stage of Growth*

THE IMPORTANCE OF FEELING
IMPORTANT

Before we begin, I ask that you do one thing. I ask that you empower yourself by believing one very crucial piece of information: you are important. That's right, you really do matter. This is the first and foremost concept that you must accept if you hope to unearth your inner spark and reawaken the truly happy you. Many people have trouble believing this, so I'll say it again. *You are important.* Important to me, important to others, and important to the world.

If you've had trouble believing this in the past, can you choose to believe it from here on out? If so, congratulations— you've taken your first step towards your truly happy self. If you are still having trouble convincing yourself, don't despair. Just keep this fact at the forefront of your mind and keep reading.

As I was saying, I want to back up a bit and explain why a book like this came to be. I didn't just google "How to make others happy." Not at all. This book came to be because I lived it; I went on a journey to hell and back trying to find a spark—

just a little something that would show me that something better was possible. This book is the product of *a lot* of sweat, tears, sorrow, relief and joy. The ideas here are direct results of my own personal struggles with things like self-love, self-worth and an overall sense of true happiness. I worked hard to get to this place of healing and acceptance, and with my experience and wisdom, I want to help make it easier for you to get there, too.

This is not an ordinary self-help guide. In a sea of books about happiness and rejuvenation, you'll see that this one is not written by a psychologist or a guru, but rather a normal person who woke up one day and decided to do things differently—for better or for worse. I understand that it's not easy to accept that you are important if you haven't felt that way in a long time. I understand that it's not easy to welcome self-change with open arms, especially if you are guilty, like I was, of holding yourself to insurmountable standards.

I am a thirty-something wife, mother, daughter, sister and friend. I'm not anyone famous (although I like to think I could be when I put on my fancy clothes). After receiving a bachelor's degree in communications media, I went on to pursue a more satisfying career as a registered dental hygienist. I also have a hearing disability; with severe to profound hearing loss in both ears, I have worn hearing aids since I was about six years old. I rely heavily on lipreading, a skill my kids think is awesome and unique; they've made it into *our* special language.

I spent most of my life trying to be "normal" and fit in. I was angry that I had a disability and angry that my life was "hard." My parents divorced when I was very young, and the aftermath was challenging; I struggled with bonding and attachment issues, and I lacked good role models when it came to open, honest, happy and loving relationships. With little emotional support growing up and feeling lost in the shuffle of my split families, I developed some serious self-esteem issues. I was constantly changing who I *thought* I should be. So, of course, I always found myself asking, "What am I doing wrong?! Why don't I feel happy?"

Because of this rocky start, many people might view my adult life as an amazing success story, with my college degree, handsome husband, healthy children, good job, nice home, fancy trips. And it *is* beautiful and wonderful! But for some reason, back before my intense journey to self-discovery, all I saw was a sad, gray, incomplete life whose happy moments were always overshadowed by something just beyond my understanding.

So that brings me, again, to how I came to write this book. I didn't know what was dimming my joy, but I knew that I needed to find out. It began simply enough—by seeking professional help. Before my journey would near its end, I would work my way through three different therapists, one who introduced me to a possible diagnosis of Borderline Personality Disorder. While this diagnosis shed light on many of my perceived issues, I still felt incomplete; to me, it was just another excuse I could use for being unhappy. So, I kept searching. I immersed myself in things like meditation and yoga, Reiki and shamanic drumming sessions, hypnosis and even past-life regression. I googled lots of things and read lots of books. I highlighted, underlined and bent down important page corners, feeling confident my life would change from doing so. I studied different religions, hoping for some sort of sign or calling. I even left my "friends" on

Facebook without warning, eager to get rid of my "old way of life."

Some parts of my search propelled my healing more than others, like when I explored ancient Peruvian psychedelic medicines. These intense, spiritual and therapeutic concoctions helped guide me towards a better understanding of my ego and the utter importance of self-acceptance and enjoying my life's journey.

Other decisions I made created more chaos and uncertainty, like when I convinced myself that my husband and I did not love each other anymore and decided—for the both of us, mind you—that I should move out of our house and into an apartment of my own. This lasted several months, until my husband came down with a rare neurologic condition that kept him in severe pain for weeks. As I watched him suffer, powerless to help, I was left wondering if it was my recent actions that had brought upon the illness. Luckily, after many months working with a physical therapist and with his strong determination, my husband made a full recovery. While we never had a clear understanding of what actually caused his illness or why it happened, it left a pretty big impression on us both. We found ourselves asking some serious questions like: do life, love and marriage really have to be hard, or had we just been missing the point of it all?

In the end, we chose to fight harder for our marriage and found our way back to one another, becoming much closer than before. As a result of this choice, my husband and I have pledged to start creating a new story together.

However, this experience with my husband proved to me that, in the wake of my depression, I wasn't the only one being tested. There were times that I was selfish, stubborn and mean as I was fighting and clawing my way through one experience after another. I left many family members and friends feeling confused and helpless as I scrambled to find a light within my darkness.

But what I didn't do, as you'll see, is give up.

And finally, a spark did emerge.

Before this journey, I would have never attempted to write a book or create a blog and website. I didn't use Twitter, Instagram, Snapchat or any other social media besides Facebook and Pinterest. But here I am, publishing a book for all the world to see. All because I finally found my way home. I rediscovered my inner spark of joy and have since become passionate about inspiring others to love themselves and the life they live.

So, if you take nothing else away from this, know, at least, that this book is written from the heart. There are so many people out there struggling, and if I can help convince even just one person that they are meant for joy, then my own struggles will be worth that much more. I want to be a lifeline to those who need it the most. With this book, I want to help you see past all the gloom and doom to the real beauty that surrounds you. Once your field of vision is clear, you will start to feel the sun on your face, and you will feel that spark of joy deep in your core. You'll find that your "something missing" wasn't really missing after all. And the joy and the laughter will come again. And the journey towards your true self will begin.

3

"Happiness can be found, even in the darkest of times, if one only remembers to turn on the light." —J.K. Rowling, *Harry Potter and the Prisoner of Azkaban*

WHAT IS HAPPINESS?

.

"Happiness" means something different to everyone. What's more, once we experience it, we all feel it in different ways. We can work towards understanding the complexities of this sought-after emotion by looking at the difference between feeling emotionally happy and feeling mentally happy.

The *emotional* experience of feeling happiness is heavily dependent on one's current mood, thoughts and feelings. And like those things, emotional happiness comes and goes rather easily. Often, we think we need to feel happy all the time, and in striving to fill this perceived need, we seek out a continuous flow of stimuli even though the pleasure it brings is fleeting. This constant searching eventually wears us down and ultimately just makes us feel more unhappy.

Whereas experiencing *mental* happiness, or what I consider true happiness, is best described as one's contentment with life in general. It's being able to find enjoyment and pleasure in the things you do and with the people around you.

It's also about feeling good day-to-day and being able to rebound quickly when confronted with challenging emotions or situations. This state of happiness is more deep-seated, long-lasting and often goes hand-in-hand with feelings of inner peace.

It is this mental happiness that should carry the most weight. This type of true happiness, or true joy, is felt at the core of your being, and it's what you should strive to understand the most. What brings you joy—and how you embrace that joy—is what makes it unique to you. While true happiness is ever-present, it can often be hidden under layers of our own self-doubt. I hope to show you how to identify those layers so your true happiness can shine through. Like a hug from a long-lost friend, your true joy has always been right there waiting for you to embrace it.

So, let me be clear. I want you to succeed. I want you to feel happy, truly happy. I want you to realize that it is possible to love who you are—to love your life, accept your past, look forward to today, and feel confident in tomorrow. To be thankful, loving and kind to your family, friends and strangers. I want you to realize that even when you feel dark and empty, you, too, have a spark glowing within.

Let's go discover the truly happy you.

4

"Every child is an artist. The problem is how to remain an artist once he grows up." —Pablo Picasso

PURSUE YOUR PASSIONS

One of the most important things you can do for yourself, and for your overall state of mind, is to pursue the things you are most passionate about. For many of us, discovering what we are truly passionate about may not come easily. But setting out to find one or more interests that inspire feelings of happiness, fulfillment, gratitude and contentment is a task worth undertaking, for they are among the strongest tools to finding the truly happy you.

If you had asked me after my high school graduation to list my passions, my answer would have been: spending time with my boyfriend, sleeping as much as possible and choosing a college to attend that was far away from home. I didn't know what I wanted to do with the rest of my life, but I thought these three things, at least, were worth accomplishing.

By the time my first summer break rolled around, I was feeling less than stellar about where these passions were getting me. My boyfriend wanted to see other people and started dating the girl in a dorm room down the hall; my report card, and subsequent academic probation, suggested I was sleeping *too* much; and the drive back home was a moot point, as I needed to attend summer classes if I wanted to continue my college education at all!

Over the next three years, I changed majors three times, ultimately walking across the big stage to receive a rolled-up piece of paper representing my degree in communications media. I felt accomplished, yet unsure of what I was going to do next. Two unfulfilling years later, I finally allowed myself to face the truth.

I really wasn't passionate about the career path I had chosen.

By this time, I was married and was pressuring myself to find a "good, respectable job." Performing data entry in a large, windowless clothing warehouse was not something that inspired pride. I wanted a job that made a difference in the world, and one that, in my opinion, held some prestige. So, I did what anyone would do when faced with such an important decision...I searched for answers in the classified section of my city newspaper! True, it might not have been the most reliable way to find a dream, but two and a half years later, I walked across the stage again to begin a new career as a registered dental hygienist.

I've been a practicing dental hygienist for over ten years now. Do I love what I do? For the most part, yes. Am I passionate about what I do? Maybe not as much as I sometimes wish I was. I definitely feel that I accomplished my goal of obtaining a "respectable" job, and I think this career choice was a step in the right direction. It just might not be my true passion, because, to be honest, I feel I am still working to uncover more of what that is. However, my new career has become a big part of my life story by allowing me to help others.

Much of my enjoyment as a dental hygienist comes from the non-clinical aspects of my job. When I have a patient in my operatory chair, we often discuss more than just dental issues. While I may educate them about oral health and preventative care, they educate me about life by trusting me and confiding in me enough to share their stories. Sometimes, our appointments feel more like therapy sessions—although I include that therapy free of charge, of course! So, for the most part, I enjoy what I do.

Some time ago, before this recent journey of mine, I became obsessed with measuring people's general levels of job satisfaction. I wanted to see if there were other people, like me, who may not have chosen a career that they were truly passionate about. I envisioned using surveys to compile information about the wide array of unique jobs available. I'd investigate what criteria and/or schooling was needed for each, along with the recommended skills and personality traits, the average salary, and the potential for travel and advancement. I wanted to see how many people out there actually had their "dream job," and for those who didn't have it, what they were doing instead. A book with information like this could have saved me a ton of money and heartache back when I was eighteen and looking for my forever career.

It turns out that finding and following our passions is not as common as one might think. I have had the opportunity to talk to a lot of people over the past few years, and I've found that for most people, their job is just that: a job. Many told me that their job was "okay" or said "it pays the bills." Some mentioned that while they enjoyed their job, it often came at a price—long hours, poor work-life balance or low pay. Some stated outright that they just "sucked it up" day in and day out. It turned out that the desire for a good, stable, high-paying job overshadowed the need to find something that spoke to a person's true passions.

This was all pretty disappointing. So many people compromising on their happiness. I only had one person who used the words "my dream job." He worked for the K-9 unit of the Secret Service.

So...what can *you* do if you have less than stellar feelings about waking up to another day on the job? Let's try an activity.

Grab a pen and paper. Begin by making a (slightly modified) pros and cons list about your current job; in three separate columns, list the things that you love, the things that you like, and the things that you really dislike.

Wondering what to put in your "love" and "like" columns? Perhaps it's the people you work with who make your day fun, energizing and rewarding. Maybe it's that you get to work outside and enjoy a change of scenery each day. You might love your job's predictability or, conversely, love how it's fast-paced and always brings a new challenge. Write down anything that makes you say, "Hey, I like that!" in one of those two columns.

Moving on to that last column, the things that you don't enjoy so much, what are some of the things that make you cringe? Could it be annoying or unproductive coworkers, long hours, or an overly demanding boss? Maybe the salary is not enough for the work you put in, or maybe the benefits could be better. Write all these things down as well.

As you study the lists you've made, what patterns emerge? Does a long list of pros help you see your job in a brighter light? Are you reminded of why you initially chose your career? Or do you see that your cons list is disappointingly long? Once you begin to identify both your job's positive points as well as its negative ones, you are already on your way to creating change. These lists can help you decide just what type of change you need, what areas to focus on, and in what ways you could go about ensuring greater enjoyment at work.

You can also, now, use these lists to help brainstorm some possible solutions for achieving greater job satisfaction. Can you ask for a raise? Would you take a pay cut and work fewer hours if it meant more free time for yourself? Or is it possible to try something completely new? Can you take some online courses to work towards a career advancement? Or would you like to branch out to a different department or even a different employer? Do you think you have what it takes to try your hand at something completely unrelated? Maybe your true passion lies elsewhere, in uncharted territory.

Now, you might feel like you have no real passion for anything and that you wouldn't be able to find some if your life depended on it. Ease your anxieties by getting a new piece of paper and trying the following technique.

Begin by making two columns this time. On one side, list the activities that you are interested in. These are things that you like to do or *would* like to do if you had the free time. It might include things like:

- Sailing
- Organizing
- Travel
- Exercise
- Sewing
- Animals
- Writing

Now, in the next column, list skills that you excel at—or maybe you aren't an expert at these things, but you are darn good! Even skills from your current job can go here. That column may look like this:

- Graphic/video design
- Photography
- Finance/budgeting
- Management
- Animal care
- Teaching
- DIY repair work

Study the two sides. What connections can you see? Maybe you could be an animal/pet photographer. Or you could work with sailboat charter companies doing graphic design and video editing for their marketing division. How about teaching and/or writing online courses on how to better manage technology companies? Maybe you will see a new business idea or something you could turn into a creative, money-making hobby.

Whatever it is that you choose to call your job, strive to find the passion in it. If you discover that you want something more, I encourage you to pursue that at all costs. Ultimately, if you do what you love, then you will love what you do! You don't need a degree in rocket science to know that this is a recipe for living a happier, more fulfilled and more passionate life!

5

"Our future is created from choices we make in every moment." —Deepak Chopra

.

TAKE A STAND AGAINST INDECISION

Oftentimes, making decisions and standing behind them is difficult, especially if you feel insecure. We live in a world full of options and choices, making it easy for anyone to become overwhelmed. This type of feeling can be frustrating and can allow bad habits to set in, such as letting others make decisions for you. There's a reason that terms like "helicopter parent" and "micromanager" exist. Nowadays, it's easier than ever to fall into patterns of indecision.

Still, making our own decisions is an important part of developing a strong sense of self. When we can do this, no matter how simple or trivial, we feel stronger and more confident. We feel in control of our own life, and that encourages a sense of peace and comfort deep within our core. Whether our decisions turn out to be good or not so good, we nevertheless will learn something from them and grow— intellectually, emotionally, spiritually and in many other ways. This growth is key to building not only a strong sense of self-worth but self-confidence as well.

Often, we are left feeling lost, powerless and even angry when our independence gets tested. The response of a toddler who doesn't want to get dressed in the morning is a good example. Also, remember earlier when I shared about my decision to move out of my house? A large part of that decision-making process stemmed from the need to feel empowered and in control of my life during a time when I was feeling the most out-of-control. Making firm decisions—even bad ones—can still bring about positive change in the end.

Let me share an example of how someone—specifically, my nine-year-old son—becomes empowered when given the right to choose.

My son was born with a smile on his face and a key to my heart. He is the first light of my life. Sensitive, thoughtful and always the first to forgive and forget, he is full of gratitude and especially loves sharing the "little moments" in life with family and friends, whether that means enjoying our big holiday gatherings or the simple way I tuck him in each night by creating a "bubble" with his blanket and letting it cascade down around him. He is hardly afraid to talk about his thoughts and feelings and he is as insightful as ever, but, regrettably—and mostly through the fault of us, his parents— he tends to put a lot of expectations on himself. The fear of failure and disappointment can often leave him paralyzed with frustration.

My son had been training in the Korean martial art known as Tae Kwon Do (TKD) for the past four years, and, after working his way through level after level of belt mastery, he finally had the ultimate black belt in his sights!

His father and I were ecstatic, of course. He had worked so hard, from the evening training sessions he had during preschool all the way through numerous after-school sessions, summer camps and tournaments. With so many hours already logged, I figured he would breeze right on through this milestone.

Not quite. Four years in, he began to express feelings of burnout and an unwillingness to go to practices. We understood where his feelings were coming from, but we had hopes that being so near a potential "finish line" would lift his spirits enough that sheer determination could carry him through.

However, determination wasn't enough. The TKD Masters informed my son that there would be additional practices on Saturdays in order to ensure that students met the strict criteria for the final testing. Black belt training is an honor; as my husband likes to say, "They don't just hand out black belts to anybody that wants one. You have to earn it."

This was not what my son wanted to hear. He cried and whined. He sulked, becoming more defiant with us on a daily basis. At first, my husband and I were angry and disappointed. Didn't we deserve some credit and appreciation? We were about to plop down hundreds of dollars for him to take this test, not to mention all the time and money we had already invested over the years. How could he be acting like this? He was so close to the end—how could he just give up so easily? We didn't raise a quitter.

But wait. Why were we making this about us?

This was about our little boy, a young person who has the same desires to feel in control of his own life as we do. He just wanted to be a kid, playing with friends or on his Xbox. However, communicating his frustrations to us was hard, because he did not want to disappoint us.

My husband and I talked about this realization privately. Afterwards, we called our son to join us for a family meeting and opened the lines of communication with him in a very calm and open-minded way. We let him talk. We acknowledged his feelings and let him know that all of those feelings were okay. We informed him that he was free to make his own decisions on how he wanted to navigate through this challenging time. We also assured him that we were not angry or upset with him, and that we would fully support any decision he made.

Once we empowered him to make the choice himself, we could see a change. He started thinking out loud, sharing that he was tired of doing TKD all the time and how he sometimes wanted to quit. While he had concerns about failing the test, he could also imagine what it would feel like if and when he finally received his black belt.

Although we did not expect him to make his decision that night, he did. After talking things through, and using us as a positive sounding board, he decided he wanted to push forward. He wanted to be a black belt in Tae Kwon Do.

After that night, we saw a new level of confidence rise within him, and we could see that he was enjoying himself at practices again. He still had times of frustration, but he was committed to following through with the decision he had made. The pride he has now while wearing his well-earned black belt is priceless.

Reflecting back on this time, I am able to see that this was not only a life lesson for him, but one for me as well. Although my son is still too young to make *all* of his own decisions, this was a great step in learning self-reliance and self-confidence. And I am so glad we shared this lesson together.

Do you find yourself struggling with indecision? Do you crave more control or self-confidence in your own life? Are you fighting to assert your independence, yet still cower with hesitation? Maybe you have parents who continue to infantilize you or overbearing bosses and workaholic coworkers. Maybe your partner is controlling or narcissistic, or your own self-doubt is running the show. Regardless of where the struggle comes from, further apprehension will only continue to hold you back from living a more autonomous life.

Can you identify some areas in your life where you could empower yourself by making your own choices? First and foremost, don't wait for someone else to make them for you. Take control of that work project you've put so much effort into. Make your voice heard when you and your partner debate future financial plans. Do you want to order the cheeseburger and fries instead of a salad at lunch? Do it. Are you driving to the in-laws' house for the holiday and want to take the scenic route? Take it! See what will happen if you start saying "yes" more and "I don't know" less.

Now, think about the story of my son from another perspective. Are there people in *your* life who could benefit from more independence? For example, perhaps you have a tendency to be that "micromanager" with your office staff. Could you entrust them with tasks or projects and not hover over every detail? Do you have an open-door policy for questions or concerns? Can you provide positive feedback as well as constructive criticism?

Would others describe you as a "helicopter parent?" Is it your way or the highway when it comes to parenting? Do you have strict rules for just about everything? Could you try to "hover" less and allow your child to "choose" more?

All of us have the right to make decisions about how we live our life, as every new decision is a building block towards greater self-worth and emotional strength. Feel confident in your decisions, because with that comes pride. And having pride in the things you do, and in yourself in general, will create more self-worth, more self-love and an independence that's worth fighting for.

Do you have what it takes to take a stand against your own indecision? You should answer that with a resounding, "Yes!"

6

"Some people awaken spiritually without ever coming into contact with any meditation technique or any spiritual teaching. They may awaken simply because they can't stand the suffering anymore." —Eckhart Tolle, *A New Earth: Awakening to Your Life's Purpose*

RELEASE THE ANCHORS TO YOUR PAST PAINS

Amazingly, one of the most profound things that happened to me during this journey happened at a time when I didn't think things could be worse, mentally, physically, or emotionally. I was in the middle of my soul-searching journey, and I was getting scared, as I still had more questions than answers—or so it seemed at the time.

I made a desperate appointment with what was to be my third therapist of this story. They say that the third time's a charm, right? By now I was ready to try anything, even pharmaceuticals. Before, I had been adamant that I did not want to resort to prescription medication, as I felt it would put a label on me that shouted, "She's not perfect!" But now I felt like I was running out of options. Maybe I needed a little pill to help me rebound.

When my appointment day arrived, I walked in the door feeling confident. I was certain that I knew just what to say; I had, after all, talked through my "problems" with countless therapists over the years. With any luck, she'd know just the right pill to make me all better. I was putting a lot of expectations on a stranger. Was I wrong to be so hopeful?

The doctor welcomed me and sat across the room. She had her pad and pencil ready, which I thought was a good sign. Jumping right in, she began with the usual, "Tell me what brought you here today." I tried to find the words that would explain my thoughts, feelings and reasons why I was on her couch that day. To my surprise, my eyes began to well up, and I gave her my life story in between the tears, sniffles and half-sobs.

I told her how I had felt like driving my car into a concrete wall. How I thought that, by having real physical wounds, it would be easier for others to understand the darkness I felt inside. I tore open the old wounds from my childhood and offered the "why me?" refrain of my hearing disability. I shared how I was still mourning past relationships that had left me with a broken heart and wondered why I hadn't been able to love them the right way. I told her how I felt lonely despite my full and busy life, and I expressed my lack of confidence about being a good mother and wife, as I was sure my family deserved better. I remember trying to explain the feeling of not knowing who I truly was deep down.

Not much of what I was saying seemed to faze her—at least not how I was expecting it to. She seemed impatient, although she mentioned that she was feeling sick and issued her apologies. I began to worry; if she wasn't feeling one hundred percent, how was I ever going to get what I came for?

She offered her thoughts and concerns about my health and safety. Once she felt that I was stable enough to continue, she started digging deeper into my psyche. Little did I know what was about to happen next. It was the spark that would ultimately save my marriage, the one that would reawaken my role as a mother, and the one that would truly help turn the page of my story. The sun was about to come out from behind the clouds, and its light would burst through to my darkness and illuminate my soul. One question and *bang!*

She asked: "How long ago did most of these things that you are holding on to take place?"

"A while ago," I replied, a weird feeling starting to churn in my gut.

She pressed me for a more definitive answer.

"Something like twenty years ago, maybe."

"Twenty years ago?" she repeated, matter-of-fact.

It was like a lightning bolt cracked down. Suddenly, the darkness began to clear from my mind. *Twenty freakin' years ago!* Really?! Twenty *years!* Doesn't this seem silly to you? If I ever needed an example of what an "ah-ha!" moment was, well this was it! An "Ah-ha! I really am a fool!" moment.

How could I have let these things tie me down for so incredibly long? How much of my life had I missed while allowing these demons from my past to steal my right to happiness?

I began to question my real identity. If I wasn't my demons, who was I? Maybe—no, surely—I was a far better person than I had believed. I realized that I didn't have to be the victim anymore. While I certainly did not have to like everything that happened in the past, I sure as hell did not need to waste one more minute letting those anchors drag me down. I was ready to discover who I could be without them. I was ready to be a bigger, brighter and happier me. Right here, right now.

One simple question, and these thoughts exploded in my

mind like fireworks. From that moment, I knew I had severed those chains to my past. I was finally floating free, with a newfound awareness that my missing spark of joy had never been missing at all.

Remember the magic pill I thought I needed? Wouldn't you say I got what I came for? No prescription required!

I never saw that therapist again.

What traumatic or challenging events from your past are still holding on to you? Do these things weigh on your mind more often than you'd like? What chains are you allowing to squeeze the breath out of you? Would you like to enjoy a life without those heavy weights?

Then I challenge you to ask yourself the very same question that this therapist asked me: "How long ago?" Maybe you will also see that your past is just that—the past. While you can't change it, and you may not like it, you can choose to accept it for what it is. You can choose to thank the past for being a part of your story and then say goodbye. Empower yourself to make the choice to move forward. This is your journey. Use your past stories and memories as a tool to serve you in a positive, uplifting way.

Aren't you tired of suffering? Anchors aweigh!

7

"Nature does not hurry, yet everything is accomplished." —Lao Tzu, *Tao Te Ching*

FIVE SENSES TO HAPPINESS

Most of us have been blessed with five unique and amazing ways to experience this life we live: sound, smell, taste, sight and touch. Sadly, we are so accustomed to these unique abilities that we often take them for granted. We have allowed our five senses to become white noise, easily tuned out.

In this chapter, I will challenge you to fully immerse yourself in each one. I will discuss them individually and give examples and suggestions on ways to bring their beauty back into your life. However, before we get started, I'd like to take a moment to introduce mindfulness. In this chapter, mindfulness simply means bringing your full attention to the given moment. While I devote an entire chapter to mindfulness later in the book, it's also an important part of being able to truly appreciate your five senses.

Let's begin your journey of the five senses to happiness with a few mindful exercises. Allow yourself to fully experience each of the following five sections by spending a few minutes on each one.

Sense of Hearing:

Let's focus on our ears. Start with something simple, like listening to music. But before you hit play on your favorite Pandora or Spotify station, look at what's on the playlist—you want to make sure that what you choose is appropriate for this type of activity. I suggest that you stay away from songs with really heavy lyrics; songs with messages about violence, degradation, addiction, revenge, broken hearts, or remembering loved ones who have passed are *not* the type of songs you want for this exercise.

Instead, choose playlists that offer music with positive and empowering lyrics. Better yet, find music with uplifting sounds, such as classical, jazz, and film scores. Or maybe try listening to something new, like the sounds of Tibetan singing bowls. As you're listening, remember that you want to focus on really hearing each sound.

Here's another idea for the next time you are in a bookstore or the local coffee shop. Just close your eyes and listen, processing the sounds around you. Listen to the low murmur of conversations and laughter. Hear the steam hissing from the espresso machine, the loud whir of the coffee grinder, the clink of ice in a glass or the ding of silverware stirring in a cup.

How about when you are sitting outside in your neighborhood? Can you make out the sound of birds chirping in the trees, a lawn mower running or cars driving down the street? Do you hear heels clicking on the sidewalk or a siren racing away? What about the wind? Can you hear that, too?

What are the sounds of *your* world? What are some emotions you felt while focusing on your sense of hearing? What can you hear now that you are really listening?

Sense of Smell:

Now, let's focus on our nose. The next time you head outside to check the mail or walk the dog, take a moment to pause and lift your nose to the air. Can you smell the subtle sweetness in the air following a fresh rainstorm? Or the smoke from the neighbor's grill? Can you smell the dumpster funk from the alley down the block, or maybe the particular thickness of your city's air in summer? Take a moment to smell the flowers you pass along your way. When is the last time you actually stopped to smell the roses, anyway? Enjoy it!

How about when you arrive at home in the evening? Is your significant other on dinner duty? Do you smell the food cooking before you walk in the front door? Can you almost taste the spices and herbs? When your loved one meets you at the door, can you detect the subtle scent of their cologne or perfume? Or does a whiff of shampoo pass your nose as you go in for a hug?

Next, try to think of some of your favorite smells. What scents transport you back to happy childhood memories? A simple whiff of fruity or floral perfume might remind you of your mother or grandmother. Maybe the scent of bug spray takes you back to summer camp. Perhaps the smell of hot dogs and funnel cake bring back memories of the town fair and your first love.

Isn't it amazing how our mind processes and stores information like this? Something so simple, yet invisible, is powerful enough to unlock remarkable memories. So, enjoy this feat! Appreciate all that your sense of smell offers. Think about when you are sick with a cold and your nose is completely blocked. How do you think things would be different for you if you couldn't smell the world around you?

What can you smell now that you're really focused this sense?

Sense of Taste:

What's the best way to focus on your sense of taste? Why, immerse yourself in food and drink, of course! This can be a fun activity, as you will start to become more aware of how you nourish your body. The next time you sit down to a meal, try to be fully engaged.

Close your eyes and focus on the bite you're taking. Feel the smooth metal as the fork leaves your lips. Feel the food's texture as you begin to chew. Alert yourself to the different combinations of salty, sweet, sour, and bitter. As you swallow, follow the bite all the way down to your stomach before going in for another. I want you to feel how lucky you are at that moment to be able to enjoy that food.

It's also important to consider how invested you are in the foods that you buy and consume. Let's say that you frequent the local coffee shop. You might typically spend about five dollars there each day. Why do you choose to make this five-dollar coffee purchase when you could have just as well made a cup at home? There may be several reasons why you would use your hard-earned money for a small reward. Perhaps it provides comfort during the morning rush or offers you a much-needed afternoon pick-me-up.

Still, whatever your reason is for making that purchase, ask yourself if it has become so routine that you've forgotten its real value. The same goes for any meal you indulge in at restaurants, or ingredients that you purchase from the grocery store to prepare a meal at home. The more importance you place on your food and drink, the more satisfied you will feel. Every time we engage ourselves in choosing, buying, preparing, sharing, and, most importantly, consuming food and drink, we are creating long-lasting moments to be valued.

Sure, it might sound like a bit much—and I'm sure your boss wouldn't understand a two-hour lunch break to focus on "really tasting my meal!"—but if trying it once enables you to appreciate what you consume a little bit more, then it was worth it.

What are some special moments in your life, past or present, that may revolve around food or drink? Are these moments celebrations, religious practices, times of mourning or simply an everyday event? Are there times when you indulge in a feast, or perhaps, you prepare yourself for a fast? How do you feel during these moments?

What more can you taste when you are really focused on tasting?

Sense of Sight:

Let's move on to our eyes. This may seem like an easy challenge, but many people are walking around blind to the world and to the life they are living.

First and foremost, be aware of your surroundings. If

you're outside, watch leaves sway in the breeze or the sun set behind the tallest city building. Watch the squirrels dancing up and down the trees. Become mesmerized by raindrops as they bounce on the pavement or fluffy snowflakes as they make their slow descent from the sky.

You should also do some people watching. Observe how your loved ones spend their time. See how they interact with their life. Focus in on their facial expressions and movements. Watch their body language and see how they experience emotions such as frustration, wonder, sadness or joy.

Other parts of encouraging visual awareness include making more of your indoor spaces. Beautifying the world around you can be an overall mood-booster. Big, colorful artwork or ornate decorations offer something meaningful and unique to enjoy, while hanging personal photographs, choosing paint with warm hues, and adding soft white lights to illuminate a room can all work to create tranquility.

How does it feel to be a full-time observer? Can you see just how slow and unassuming the world is when there are no clocks being watched? What emotions does it stir up?

What can you see when you are really focused on seeing?

Sense of Touch:

Click-clack, click-clack. Was I fully focused on each computer key as I typed this sentence? Not really, no. But what happens when I call my attention to it? As I start pressing the keys, I feel the pads of my fingers push against the smooth tiles, followed by a slight pulsation as I release. The energy lingers after each one, but all of this is easily filtered out when I am not focused on it.

Now you try. Focus on your sensations of touch. Can you feel your bum getting numb right now from sitting in the same spot while you're reading? If you go outside can you feel the warmth of the sun on your face or the slight chill of raindrops as they slide down your skin? Focus on feeling the soft cotton of your clothing or the feathering of hair against your cheek. Take off your socks and shoes and feel the cool dampness of the earth beneath your feet.

How about when you have guests arriving for an impromptu get together, can you feel the cool brass handle of the door as you open it? Now, how will you greet your guests? Do you extend a hand, give a quick kiss on the cheek or go in for a warm hug? Each greeting plays on our sense of touch. Hugging, in particular, involves a huge amount of closeness and has even gotten a lot of press lately for all the positive health benefits that it can offer.

Lastly, while focused on your sense of touch, put your hand over your heart and feel your heartbeat. No words needed here. It's a miraculous and humbling thing to feel.

How did you feel during this exercise? Was it relaxing, or perhaps, did it make you uneasy? If it's the latter, reflect on that for a bit. Consider what you really feel when you are completely focused on your sense of touch.

Congratulations! You've done it. You've experienced each of your five senses to their fullest capacity. How do you think your life would be different without one, or more, of your five senses? What will you take away from this exercise? And how can you use these things to enhance your journey toward a happier, more peaceful you? Don't filter out these important things as white noise. While you may have to make a concerted effort each day to enjoy your five senses, hopefully, after this chapter, you have come to realize that they can bring quite a bit of joy.

8

"Ego says, 'Once everything falls into place, I'll feel peace.' Spirit says, 'Find your peace, and then everything will fall into place.'" —Marianne Williamson

SILENCE THE EGO AND SPEND QUALITY TIME ALONE

As important as it is to have friends and family to help fulfill you emotionally, mentally and spiritually, spending time alone is equally important. Everyone can benefit from having a little time to themselves on a daily basis. We need this time to decompress after a busy day or just to feel refreshed and renewed. A small break can allow you to refocus your energy and ponder any questions that may be weighing you down. A little solitude ultimately allows us to better control our environment and how we choose to deal with it.

During my own journey, I realized I was not making alone time a priority. Specifically, I needed to find a way to decompress after work.

My office is only four miles from my home. I never have to worry about traffic, and I am always close by if one of my kids becomes ill at school. Even if I hit all the lights, it's only a ten-minute drive. Sounds stress-free, doesn't it? Still, for some reason, I was pulling into the driveway every night cranky and annoyed.

Was it my job, or was it something else making me so unhappy? I knew I needed to investigate further. What I found were two key insights: one, my commute to and from work was too short, and two, I was allowing my ego to have a field day with my emotions.

Ego. That little voice in our head. Our inner dialogue partner. The narrator of our life story. A friend or foe?

Ever since I can remember, that little voice has constantly questioned my every move and thought. Over time, its chatter seemed to get louder and louder, and I succumbed to its gross negativity. While my ego didn't really know what other people around me were thinking, it was more than willing to make guesses, even while doing something as simple as running to the grocery store after work. It would insist that every other shopper was disappointed in the fact that I was "choosing" to leave my kids at daycare instead of bringing them along with me. I could "hear" them labeling me as an uncaring mother who did not have her priorities straight.

My ego also whispered comments about how my children —toddlers at the time—were feeling. Even though they couldn't tell time, they were also disappointed in me for leaving them at daycare longer than necessary. I "heard" them question why I did not love or care about them enough to pick them up sooner. Furthermore, my ego insisted that, in every minute spent without my children, some incredible, monumental milestone was happening, and I was, of course, missing it.

Ironically, my ego topped all of this off by assuring me that everything that it had just told me was completely ridiculous, and now, so was I. "Why can't you be more like your husband? He's not bothered by such silly things," it would say. "But he will be very disappointed in you when you arrive home tonight, so you best prepare yourself for that."

By the time I got home, not only was I stressed-out, I was full of guilt and resentment. As we spent the evening rushing from one thing to the next—sports, dinner, homework—I carried those unresolved feelings. As the eight-o'clock bedtime rolled around, I was maxed-out on patience and way overdue for some much-needed alone time. I was so busy yelling for everyone to get into bed that I even found excuses to skip storytime, just so I could have a moment to myself. My mind and body were screaming for a rest, but I couldn't, or wouldn't, hear it.

I had so many pent-up emotions that I couldn't even see how my mental exhaustion was causing my loved ones to suffer as much as I was. This sabotage wasn't fair to any of us.

Luckily, I realized that I could change this. First, I took a few steps back and I became more aware of how controlling I had let my ego become. Simply acknowledging that fact began to strip it of its power and quieted its obsessive negative chatter.

Secondly, I figured out that if I rewarded myself with some quality alone time after work, I'd arrive home with a calmer, more peaceful attitude. This period of quiet solitude would give me time to transition from the working-mother me to mommy-wife me. Realizing that I need—and deserve—some quality time alone has worked wonders for me personally, and I know my family can see the difference as well.

Are you feeling huge amounts of stress, but can't seem to identify a reason why? Do you have a controlling ego that puts a negative spin on things in your life that should be simple? Could you benefit from some extra breathing room or a transitioning period?

You can begin to find clarity by honoring yourself with some time to decompress and acknowledging that a negative ego does not properly serve you, nor does it help further your search for true happiness. Work to re-train your ego so that it offers a more positive and encouraging inner dialogue. Only when the ego becomes quieter will you be able to look more deeply within yourself for the key insights that will continue to push you forward on your journey.

Happiness is truly just a quiet mind and a quiet space away.

9

"When one door closes, another opens; but we often look so long and so regretfully upon the closed door that we do not see the one that has opened for us." — Alexander Graham Bell

"AH-HA" MOMENTS

Earlier, I wrote about an "ah-ha" moment that I experienced during what would become a life-changing therapy session. I want to explain this phenomenon a little more, because recognizing these unique moments can prove pivotal on your own journey as well.

An "ah-ha" moment is one that is truly remarkable. It's an unexpected moment in time that, once identified, has the power to rock you to the core and change the course of your life. While some "ah-ha" moments may click right away, others may not be as obvious.

Think back to the chapter about releasing your anchors to the past. Remember how my therapist asked me how long I had been holding on to my sufferings? You remember what my answer was, don't you? Twenty years. That's right, for twenty years I was holding on to things that I could not change. It was that split-second realization, that "ah-ha" moment, that made me face my current state in all its guts and glory. By choosing to empower this moment, it opened the floodgates for me to heal, washing away the mud and filth that I had been standing in for so long.

I left that therapy appointment feeling liberated. How ridiculous it was to hold onto pain for twenty years. After that "ah-ha" moment, I found myself asking more tough questions. Questions like:

- How did I let myself get consumed by such negativity?
- Why did I allow my ego to hold me captive in self-doubt and self-sabotage?
- How much happiness and beauty had I missed out on?

I knew right then that I did not want to waste another precious second wondering how things *could*, or *should*, have been. I allowed my "ah-ha" moment to be my teacher, to lead me toward living my life in a more mindful way—one where I am more appreciative and focused on the *present moments*.

I am sure that you have heard about other famous "ah-ha" moments that have inspired, saved or influenced someone's life. Maybe you are one of the lucky ones, like me, and have had a pivotal "ah-ha" moment or two of your own. If you have, then you know just how hard it is to describe it to others, because it almost sounds unbelievable. How do you put into words the feeling when that lightbulb clicks on, and *boom!* you're seeing things clearly? How do you describe those fireworks? Or that moment when your core explodes with such enormous energy, strength, light and joy?

As you might imagine, I don't talk much about my "ah-ha" moments, as I worry about coming off as an egocentric know-it-all. But given the power realizing their importance can have, I knew that I needed to share it with others in some way. And here we are.

Do you feel like you need more direction in your life? Are you wondering if you may have missed an "ah-ha" moment of your own? The best way to find those answers is to get out your magnifying glass and put on some strong body armor. You'll need to rehash some of your most challenging moments and events—hence the need to come prepared—and go over them with a fine-toothed comb. If you can remain detached from those memories and refrain from getting caught up in past emotions, you may be able to see something new. What can you discover by shining a brighter light on your darkness? Do you see a lesson that could be given more power in your life? Is there a hard truth that can be faced? Are there new paths for you to explore?

If you have been lucky enough to experience an "ah-ha" moment of your own, I am sure you will remember it for a long time. I hope that you have allowed it to heal you, and that you let it continue to guide you in moving forward in a positive way on your journey.

If you haven't had an "ah-ha" moment and feel like you need one, don't despair. Sometimes they need a little unearthing. Continue digging and applying the lessons I discuss here into your daily routine. Keep going and keep smiling. If you truly need an "ah-ha" moment, it will arrive when you least expect it. Only now, you'll be ready for it!

10

"Real happiness is cheap enough, yet how dearly we pay for its counterfeit." — Hosea Ballou

LESS IS MORE

Would you believe that you can have more just by having less? Believe it, because it really is true. We all seem to want "more" in our lives and will often go to extreme lengths to get it. But I have found that the more I strive to live a minimalistic life, the more satisfied I am overall.

Let me give an example. Let's say you would like to buy a new couch. The one you have is still in good condition, but you saw a catalog the other day featuring some really nice living rooms, and now you're excited for a change. You deserve a nice upgrade.

In order to save time and energy, you do a Google search and find a black leather couch that would look great in your living room. You sell yourself on the idea by saying that leather is a good, durable material, and this couch will last you a long time. Not to mention that the size is right, and its color matches the rest of your decor.

It's just that the pictures on the website make it look even more amazing with a nice blanket draped over the side and matching throw pillows. There's also a faux-fur rug gracefully laid out in front of it beneath a round, wooden coffee table. Add in the nice paintings on the walls and the beautiful recessed lighting and that seals the deal—you want that entire living room! But you only came looking for a couch. The price tag for the couch says it's five thousand dollars. Do you buy it?

Sure, it looks amazing! It would make your living room look like a Pottery Barn catalog. But ask yourself a few questions: what joy can you really get from a five-thousand-dollar leather sofa? Who sits on it? Would you let your kids be kids and jump from one cushion to the next? Can you eat ice cream cones as you watch a movie? Will you always be expecting your friends to comment on how beautiful it is? Will you be proud to have spent five thousand dollars on it, or will it collect dust because you're too nervous to let anyone near it? Could you get "more" from a less expensive couch? One that can be used without so much worry?

Here is an example of choosing to have less, when you could have more. One of the dentists that I work with has been driving the same small, old car year after year. He could very easily afford to buy a high-end car with all the bells and whistles, but the unique thing about him is that he couldn't care less how he gets from point A to point B. His little four-door 2003 Honda Civic is barely hanging on, but he doesn't mind; he's not trying to puff up his chest and say, "Look how successful I am!" Sure, maybe he could upgrade a bit more, but I think it's humbling to see such a successful person making the choice to live a simple life, unconcerned about outward appearances.

Spending money—and often money that we don't really have—to buy things like fancy living room furniture, expensive cars and large houses only brings temporary happiness. All of those things will eventually need to be replaced or repaired until, ultimately, they are just an image in an old photograph.

What doesn't get old or need replacing are the memories you create in that living room and the places you travel to in that old car. You will remember the movies you watched, the games you played, the adventures you went on, the stories you laughed about, and even the tears you wiped from your daughter's face after her first broken heart. It's the simple things that become the most important.

Do you think that you would be willing to try living a more minimalistic lifestyle? What changes could you make? What could you choose to do differently? It might be helpful to make a checklist as you begin thinking about some of these questions.

The prospect of giving things up and giving things away can seem daunting at first, so start out simple. Maybe the first step is to look through your closets and drawers for the clothes that no longer fit or have not been worn in months. Place them in black trash bags so you can't see them and have second thoughts once they are there. Then move on to the bath towels and bed sheets. Owning one extra set of each should suffice, don't you think? I already see less laundry in your future! Now, maybe you could focus on other items around the house. Are there things that are just "clutter?" Can you find a way to repurpose some of those items? Or maybe you can have a yard sale or make a stop at a donation center.

Next, work to create a stricter budget. Can you pack a lunch for work? Or, instead of pricey after-work happy hours, have friends come to your place. Skip the expensive movie theater experience and wait for those blockbusters to reach

Blu-Ray. Work diligently to pay off all debt. When all is said and done, having more money in your pockets means having the opportunity to create more memorable experiences.

Finally, if you are feeling emboldened, try minimalizing in a larger sense. Ask yourself what things you might be able to do without. Can you get rid of your cable package? So much of what we watch nowadays can be streamed straight to your television set or even on your computer. Do you have a car that you could downsize? This could lead to smaller monthly payments and less spent at the gas pump, too. Or maybe you can look into ride-sharing or taking the bus or subway to work. And if you are truly ready to cut things down to a smaller size, you can look for a smaller home.

While I, like many people, sometimes dream of winning the lottery, I try to remind myself that money won't buy me true happiness. Life is about the little moments we create and share with others, not the amount of money in our bank account.

Now—with your checklist started, aren't you ready to experience more with less?

11

"Believe you can and you're halfway there." — Theodore Roosevelt

TRY SOMETHING NEW

I ended up trying many new things over the course of my journey. Some things I tried voluntarily, like when I enrolled in classes and retreats on yoga, Reiki and meditation, or when I immersed myself in all things sailing to confront some of my biggest fears—fear of the unknown, fear of the open ocean, fear of failure and imperfection. Other new things happened because of necessity. As I was becoming more aware of what wasn't working in my life, I forced myself to take action, like when I chose to take a break from my social media in order to re-evaluate some of my support circles, or the time when I tested the waters of living the single life. I thought my happiness might have been on the other side of the fence— where the grass always seemed greener—but when going there, all I ever found was just another fence to look over.

Ultimately, as I went through this intense period of trial and error, I learned resilience. At times, I felt like a rubber band stretched to the breaking point, but with each new failure, I learned how to spring back and try again.

In this chapter, I challenge you to try something new—or, hopefully, many new things. I encourage you to step outside your comfort zone, explore the world and meet new people, even if it makes you uncomfortable. It is during our times of greatest discomfort and uncertainty that we are most open to welcoming personal change and growth. As our adrenaline flows, our senses are heightened, making us more aware of the world around us. Only when the fight or flight response starts to build can you discover where your true strengths and abilities reside.

There are countless ways to find new opportunities to pursue. There are numerous online resources, including Meetup.com, that let you find groups of like-minded adventurers. A local community college might offer classes on subjects that you may be interested in but never had the chance to try. There are yoga studios, meditation centers, cooking and language classes. Visit a new restaurant specializing in an ethnic cuisine you have never tasted before. Maybe you want to challenge yourself and start training for a marathon, or volunteer at the local homeless or battered women's shelter. Take dance lessons, join a sporting group, go for a wine tasting at the local vineyard or hike the Appalachian Trail. There are knitting classes, book clubs, even groups for board game fanatics. How about learning to fence, going on a hot air balloon ride, or taking flying or sailing lessons. Or... write a book! Now, write down three new activities that *you* would like to explore.

They might not all produce an "ah-ha" moment or lead you directly to a missing puzzle piece, but I guarantee you will feel rewarded in one way or another. With each new adventure you embark on or avenue you choose to explore, your inner spark will be fueled, and with that will come increased feelings of confidence, strength and pride.

Which something new will you try today?

12

"Everything you've ever wanted is on the other side of fear." —George Addair

ACKNOWLEDGE YOUR FEARS

While I agree with George Addair, I might take it a step further and say, "Everything you've ever *needed* is on the other side of fear." The thing that holds most people back from creating change in their life is *fear*: fear of the unknown, fear of failure, fear of being judged. If we continuously give in to those fears, we are putting a limit on our own potential. And by imposing limits on ourselves, we essentially say, "I'm not good enough." If we give up before we have even tried, we may never know just what we can achieve.

If you are reading this book, you most likely have a desire for "more" in your life. Not for "more" as in stuff, which we've already talked about, but "more" as in more emotion, more purpose, more happiness. You probably feel like something needs to change, but you just don't know what. You are certain that what you seek is hiding someplace new and different, but your fears are deterring you from discovering where.

Here's some good news. By simply acknowledging your *need* and your *desire* for change, you have already taken your first step towards making "more" happen. The simple act of *acknowledgment* forces our brain to reconsider what it may have originally labeled as a "no-go" zone. This acknowledgment will allow you to begin breaking down any barriers that are holding you back. With fewer barriers working against you, the easier it will be to begin accepting your fears and pushing past them.

My own fears held me back for a long time. When I finally started to be honest with myself and acknowledge my own need for change, my journey to healing began.

Some of my honesty knocked me over.

Some of my honesty led me down dead-end roads.

Some of that honesty hurt—mentally and emotionally.

However, if I had continued to surrender to my fears, I would not be where I am today, living life with a newfound joy, enlightenment and purpose.

Overcoming your fears is no simple feat. It takes great courage and serious strength—mental, physical and emotional. While some of your fears may be right on the surface, other, complex fears may be rooted more deeply; these can take longer to see and to recognize for what they are.

Remember how I encouraged you to step outside your comfort zone by trying new things in the previous chapter? You can apply that same philosophy here as you begin to acknowledge and face your fears.

Let's say that you are at work. Or maybe you are attending a conference or even shopping at the store. Do you find that you consciously work hard to blend in with the crowds? Do you dress very conservatively and modestly? Do you always choose to sit towards the back of the room during a meeting or lecture? Do you refrain from voicing your opinions, for fear of exposing a strong accent, a stutter or simply because you feel too nervous? Do you hold back from confidently joining in on conversations because you wish you were more knowledgeable about current events? Or maybe, do you tend to avoid excursions or other physical activities because you doubt your abilities to keep up or perform well?

If you identified with any of the above questions, as I did, you may have issues with or a fear of things like public speaking or being judged by others. Let's look at a few simple ways that you could work towards facing moments like these with more courage and confidence.

The best way to begin confronting any fear is to take baby steps forward. Start by doing little things that break from the routine of your everyday life. If you're afraid of bringing attention to yourself, start off with something easy, fun or goofy, like parting your hair a different way, wearing some funky socks to work, or approaching a stranger and talking about something simple, like the weather. You can reduce public speaking anxieties by reading books, magazines or even web articles out loud. This might sound silly, and it might feel embarrassing at first, but it can build confidence in your speaking abilities as it helps develop proper word articulation, increases vocabulary and expands your knowledge of unfamiliar subject areas. You could also enroll in some acting classes. This is a great way to meet and engage with other people in a fun and pressure-free environment. You could hire a professional speaking coach or life coach. These coaches can tailor their services to meet your needs in a very personal and encouraging way.

Finally, do not relent when you feel like "nothing" is happening. This is the moment when you should push yourself harder. Acknowledge your feelings as they present themselves, but stay focused, strong and determined. And most of all, be honest with yourself. Soon you'll feel your barriers crumbling, brick by brick, and you will break through to a more joyful and free-spirited you.

13

"If you aren't good at loving yourself, you will have a difficult time loving anyone, since you'll resent the time and energy you give another person that you aren't even giving to yourself." —Barbara De Angelis

LOVE THY SELF

I began this book by telling you that you are an important person. And I asked that you work towards believing that as you progress on your journey. I want to use this chapter to talk a little more about the importance of *truly* loving and accepting who you are.

You are an amazing and beautiful soul, one who is full of enormous potential. You have a spark within you that shines its brightest when you allow the little things in life to have a joyous meaning. You have a responsibility to yourself to live a life worth remembering.

I think a lot of people struggle to believe the things I mention in the last paragraph. Or, while those messages may have been received during childhood, they've gone cold and silent as we've grown older. But it's a mistake to assume that we can't believe in them just as much now, as adults.

Poor self-esteem took hold of me at a young age. For more years than I'd like to admit, I did not like myself. I did not feel important. I did not believe that I could become whatever my heart desired. I had given up before I even knew what I was giving up on.

Because of this, I began to feel unworthy. I felt uncomfortable when friends, teachers, strangers or even family members would pay me compliments. I shrugged them off and turned around to compliment them instead. My longing to feel like I was loved and belonged somewhere, along with the constant yearning for approval, caused a lot of inner conflict. Whenever I received things that might make me feel happy and complete, I would push them away, telling myself I did not really deserve them. It was a vicious cycle.

This negative thought pattern continued throughout my adult life only because I did not realize that I had the power to change it. During the course of my journey, I've come across many wonderful people, many of whom were also searching for something "more." On the outside, these people seemed to have everything in order. They appeared happy, or at least happier than I was, because they were friendly and smiled a lot. But as we started sharing our stories, I quickly realized that, although the little details were different, the bigger struggles were similar. We were all searching for something intangible: an invisible missing piece that we were hoping, once found, would bring us to our true happiness.

I remember a young woman who shared her story during a mindfulness retreat I attended at Yogaville in Buckingham, Virginia. I remember the tears that flowed down her cheeks as she tried to explain what brought her there that weekend.

Among other things, she said that she felt "like a bad mom." This, of course, resonated with me, as I am sure it did for many other parents in the group. I felt sad that she would think this about herself. I also felt sadness for myself, because I knew that I could very well be sharing that same story.

As I worked to process this feeling, I began to see just how powerful and controlling our own thoughts can be. Seeing how much emotional turmoil she was causing just by allowing untruths to masquerade as truths was heartbreaking. It was difficult for me to hear her story without getting tears in my own eyes. A thought came to me—were we all there that day because we believed in our own untruths?

This woman was acknowledging to herself, and to everyone in the group, that she wanted change. She was also facing her fears. She wasn't doing this because someone told her to; she was choosing this change for herself. By verbalizing her fear of not being the type of mother that she wanted to be, she was now holding herself accountable to making some changes in her life.

After the retreat was over, I made a point to share my thoughts with her. I wanted her to know that I was proud of her for taking the first step of coming to this seminar and speaking her fears and challenges aloud. I encouraged her to continue working on forgiving herself so she could gain a greater sense of self-love and acceptance.

She was extremely thankful for my kind words—I think— because it showed her that someone, a stranger even, had truly listened and said they believed in her, making her feel special and important.

Remember when I talked about those "ah-ha" moments? Remember when I mentioned that it may take a while before they become fully unearthed? Well, it took a few months before I realized that the interaction I had with this stranger was another "ah-ha" moment for me. That woman was a reflection of the part of me who doubted my strength and confidence as a mother, the part of me who had a hard time forgiving and loving myself. Now, all that advice that I was offering her became advice for me.

No two people will ever have the same journey, but I do believe that we cross paths with one another for a reason. Everyone can play a role in your story. Their role may be large or it may be small, but we can, and should, learn something from everyone we meet.

We are often our own worst enemies. We criticize, blame and doubt ourselves. But once we start to believe in ourselves, to accept our mistakes and forgive ourselves, we can truly grow in our self-acceptance and self-love. When you can truly smile on the inside, your smile on the outside becomes genuine.

What about you? What untruths have *you* allowed to masquerade as truths in your life? Write them down on a piece of paper and be sure to include how you will work to discredit them. Would you agree that you could also work more diligently to build yourself up with more positive and encouraging thoughts? When someone says, "Tell me about yourself," do you have affirming adjectives ready? What will they be? Will you be able to say, "Thank you!" after a compliment?

Pay attention to the advice that you are giving to others—if it is heartfelt, then that advice should hold true in your own life as well. Listen to yourself, trust yourself, and stay true to yourself. Choose to love yourself and joy will follow!

14

"The true secret of happiness lies in taking a genuine interest in all the details of daily life." —William Morris

MINDFULNESS

Let's now talk more about mindfulness. You have already started to incorporate this art when you worked to hone in on your five senses earlier in the book, but you cannot expect to feel truly happy unless you practice mindfulness techniques on a more regular basis.

Mindfulness, or practicing mindfulness, simply means being fully present in your current moment by giving it your full and undivided attention. Because the *purpose* of your life is happening right now.

Think on that for a moment: *The purpose of your life is happening right now.* Your past has passed and is no longer your purpose. Since the future is unknown, it can't possibly be used to define your purpose—it can only be used as the *intention* of your purpose. So, all you have left is the moment you are in right now. The purpose of your life is what you are doing right now.

Let me give two simple, perhaps even silly, examples of

how you can practice mindfulness during regular, everyday activities. First, let's try some mindful reading.

You probably have a million and one things to do today. Or do you? Right now, you've taken the time to sit a read this book, and you are giving it your full and undivided attention (at least I hope you are!). Your purpose right now is to read this book, relax and maybe learn something or feel inspired. In this current moment, you should be thinking about the words you are reading. You might feel the weight of the e-reader or book in your hands while the hum of a dishwasher runs in the background. In general, you are probably comfortable, and you are probably still. You are so engaged in this moment that your brain has created a little bubble around you. Everything outside of this little bubble has become background noise. As you are reading these words, different scenarios pop into your head about how each of these topics might pertain to your present moment. *This is mindful reading!*

Let's look at another simple example, one that I call "mindful brushing."

As a dental hygienist, I have started to use this phrase with my patients a lot. I explain that mindful brushing means to brush their teeth with a purpose. That's right! When you are brushing your teeth, the purpose of your life in those moments is to clean your teeth and gums properly. You should give your full attention to brushing your teeth well. Watch in the mirror as you brush each tooth one by one, surface by surface. Don't be fast or aggressive, and use small, circular motions. Do not allow yourself to be distracted by an overactive mind. Don't worry about what you will eat for breakfast, or what shoes will match with the pants you are wearing. Don't look at your cell phone or walk around the house—just stay focused on your present moment. By focusing your attention on your purpose (having healthy teeth and gums) and the moment (brushing your teeth well), the results will speak for themselves. *This is mindful brushing!*

Practicing mindfulness is also a great tool to help center yourself during otherwise mundane tasks. You can use mindfulness while driving, folding laundry or even preparing a speech. Welcoming your current moment helps bring a calmness to the core of your being. Acceptance of your current moment helps you enjoy what you are doing even more. By practicing mindfulness, you will find that you become less stressed and less concerned about unnecessary things. This can be extremely beneficial when dealing with people— spouses, coworkers and especially children. Mindfulness translates into patience.

What areas of your life could benefit from practicing mindfulness techniques? Your kids, your job, your daily humdrum activities? Can you challenge yourself to become more fully engaged in your present moments?

Consider the possibility, too, that there may be people or things in your life that are holding you back from being fully committed to your present moment. Maybe you have a relationship that causes unnecessary heartache or anxiety, thus keeping your mind preoccupied. Or perhaps you allow yourself to get too emotionally invested in local politics, so much so that it consumes your thoughts and becomes a source of anger and prejudice. Can you choose to say goodbye to things like this?

Saying goodbye to something that has been a powerful and consistent influence in your life may be one of the hardest things that you'll ever have to face, but in doing so, it can also make room for the mental clarity and freedom that you have been yearning for. This freedom can let you focus more of your attention on what's really important: this moment right now. Remember, the present moment is the only thing you really have any control over. So, relax—great things are happening right now.

15

"Laugh, my friend, for laughter ignites a fire within the pit of your belly and awakens your being." —Stella McCartney

MORE THAN JUST A CHUCKLE

C an you laugh out loud right now? Go ahead, try it. And more than just a little chuckle! Try a good, hearty, full-bellied laugh. Don't worry if there are people around, because that makes it even better. They might look at you a little funny, but you just keep right on laughing, because after they smile quizzically, they will start laughing, too. They are laughing because you are laughing! And even though there was no real reason for the laughter to start, now everyone is much happier than they were a few minutes ago. Good job! Happy people laugh.

Laughter is beautiful. It's also contagious. If you are feeling too shy to start a laugh track of your own, try watching some of those YouTube videos of babies laughing or a silly show like *America's Funniest Home Videos* where you just can't help but laugh along.

During my year of difficulty and confusion, when I was in that deep, dark hole thinking there was no light to be found, my deeply perceptive and inquisitive daughter asked me something that I will never forget. She asked, "Mommy, how come you never laugh?"

Are you envisioning a lightbulb right now or a flash of lightning? You should be! That was another moment for my personal "Ah-ha Moments Realized" column. Because that moment hit me hard! Sadly, my daughter was right. I hardly laughed at all. How was it that my six-year-old could see this, but I couldn't?

After shedding some tears, I started to ask myself why I wasn't laughing. I had to dig deep, but what I discovered was that laughing made me feel vulnerable, and since I already felt lost and weak, adding more vulnerability was not something I welcomed. I avoided anything that might put me in that position, including good and happy things like laughter. Remember the chapter on fear? I was so scared of feeling vulnerable that I built a thick, brick barrier around myself, hoping it would protect me from difficult emotions like this.

But what really happens to us when we build walls around ourselves? Often, it's the people closest to you who suffer. For me, it's obvious that my children were suffering by living with an unhappy mother who could seemingly never be pleased.

Knowingly or unknowingly, people who are struggling to find self-love will often keep friends and loved ones at arm's length, even though, ironically, they crave the protective warmth of an embrace or the acceptance shining from a simple smile. We don't mean to send such strong messages of apathy, but we have spent so many years building our fortresses and reinforcing their walls that breaking them down may not be so quick and easy.

Let's backtrack to the mindfulness retreat I attended at Yogaville again. While there, I had the opportunity to take a

Laughter Yoga class—that's right, a special yoga class that is focused on spontaneous laughter and movement! Needless to say, I signed myself up and laughed the whole way through. While it was uncomfortable and intimidating at first, eventually I laughed big, loud belly laughs right along with everyone else. And it felt great! Some of my walls started to chip away just thanks to this simple remedy.

Are you surprised to hear that such a unique class exists? Would you believe that there are several studies that have been done on the health benefits of laughter? According to researchers at the University of Maryland, as well as others from Loma Linda University in California, there are many positive health benefits to laughing, including reduced stress levels, improved short-term memory, and an immediate boost of mood. Something as simple as a forced chuckle or even a smile can naturally make us feel better.

More importantly, laughter is often a social thing. When we are laughing, we are usually with the friends and family who are most important to us. And we don't need a study to tell us that this is a recipe for creating happy, memorable moments.

So, go ahead, start laughing. It does a body (and mind) good.

16

"Don't you dare, for one second, surround yourself with people who are not aware of the greatness that you are." —Jo Blackwell-Preston

LOVE THE ONES YOU'RE WITH

Another factor that plays an important role in your overall level of happiness is the people you have around you. By choosing to surround yourself with positive, loving, encouraging people, it makes it easier for us to want to be those things, too.

In this chapter, I challenge you to take a close look at your life story and its cast of characters. Look closely at the people to whom you've given leading roles in each act. I want you to ask yourself some questions. Do these people make you laugh, smile, and generally feel good about yourself? Do they reach out to offer help and support when you need it? Do they encourage healthy, respectful and honest communication? Can you count on them? Do you trust them?

The point of these questions is to try to figure out if the people in your life are deserving of their roles, or if, as the director, you need to make some adjustments to your casting sheet. Remember, if you are feeling alone, lost and lacking lifelines, this is the time when you need to have total confidence in your rally team.

As I mentioned before, I believe that everyone comes into our lives for a reason, whether it's to teach us, guide us, inspire us, love us, hate us, challenge us or empower us. How long these characters continue to play their role is ultimately up to us.

It might seem that, by having a solid cast of characters, we would have a much easier time writing and acting out our story. But oftentimes we get too comfortable with the status quo and cannot see when members of our cast are slacking off or not performing well. Thus, drama ensues. It's lucky for us, then, that, as directors, we can hold new auditions if we see fit. Let me share an example of a time when I was forced to take a closer look at my own story and make changes for my own best interests.

A while back, during what would have been a dramatic climax if my life really were a screenplay, I was suffering and looking for some reprieve. I reached out to a close family member and lowered my defenses in the hopes that they could help reel me back to safety. However, instead of offering their support and encouragement as I was expecting, I was met with ridicule. They said, "This isn't all about you. Not everything is about you and what you want." These words stung, especially since I had allowed myself to be vulnerable.

Now, it's quite possible that this person had only good intentions. It's also quite possible that I caught them off-guard and they didn't have the right words of advice to offer on the spot. Still, I heard this as someone expressing disappointment in me. Hurt and desperate, I considered putting my wall back up and taking back everything I said by laughing it all off. I'd go back to pretending that I was fine, go back to pretending that my sadness wasn't real.

But, for once, I didn't.

I am very thankful for that interaction, as it helped me realize the importance of a good support circle, but at the time, it was extremely difficult to process. This isn't a book where I want to whine and complain about my past. But I feel that I need to share details about how my past has shaped who I am today for you to understand how I felt when that person said, "Not everything is about you and what you want."

As I mentioned earlier, my parents divorced when I was very young, then later re-married and started new families and new lives. Many divorced couples can work together and amicably raise their kids, but my parents were young and seemed to have a harder time getting their feet on the ground. It happens, and it is understandable. I know they had the best of intentions, and as a parent myself now, I can imagine just how difficult it must have been for them to be dealing with a new baby while also trying to make new, individual lives.

Still, some of my earliest memories involve the police being called, often to very public places, in order to help sort out custody issues. My parents would try to negotiate, often not very nicely, about which of them had visitation rights at that particular time. It's a scary thing as a small child to see police officers negotiating arguments between your parents. Even scarier is when they ask you to "choose" which parent to go home with. How does a six-year-old make that decision in good conscience?

As I got older, the dynamics of my two respective families changed, which presented its own challenges. While the police were no longer involved and there was an understanding in place regarding visitation, I still felt guilty. I still had to choose who I would spend holidays with, who would need to be inconvenienced to drive me here or there, and what I would miss during the times I was away from one family or the other. Each time I would reenter a household, I would spend an exorbitant amount of time and energy finding my role again. Years older than any of my siblings, I often felt left out. Disconnected, I didn't feel like I had any cheerleaders in my corner. And when I wasn't trying to blend in or become invisible, I was left trying to prove my worth. I spent so much energy trying to prove that I mattered.

To give credit where credit is due, my family did support me in most of the things I wanted to do. Whether it was the marching band, sports, chorus, my job at the local grocery store or just wanting to go hang out at a friend's house, they provided transportation, equipment and money for what I needed at the time. And yet I struggle to remember a time when I've felt happy, safe, loved and important all at the same time. I struggle to remember a time when everyone celebrated me, or a time when my basic emotional needs were being met. When you are a child trying to make sense of your world, you don't stop to consider, "Hey, maybe this person just isn't able to love me the way I need them to," or "Maybe they had a hard life, too. I shouldn't expect so much from them." You are not only too young to verbally communicate your needs, you are too young to know exactly what your needs are. All you know is that something just doesn't feel right inside. It feels like something is missing.

So, after decades of feeling like an outsider, where did this leave me? Didn't I deserve at least a moment where it could be all about me and what I needed just this once?

Now, let's rewind to that dramatic turning point in my story when I opened up to my trusted person. I was at my absolute weakest emotionally, treading water in the dark while wearing cement shoes and desperately grasping for a lifeline. I no longer had the energy to keep up the façade of normalcy. I needed support, love, understanding, distance—anything that would help me get back to shore.

It was during this crucial moment, when I wasn't offered the support I craved, that I realized a change was needed. I was tired of feeling alone. I was tired of trying to appear strong. I was tired of feeling sad. I was tired of never feeling good enough. *I was tired of suffering.* Now, I was ready to acknowledge my pain without letting it define my story. I was waking up and acknowledging *me!*

And so with that, I decided I needed to make a few temporary adjustments to the supporting cast of my story.

I remained strong and determined as the family member and I finished our conversation. As we parted ways, I decided that from there on out, I'd keep things between us simple, and only schedule future time together for when I was mentally prepared to handle it.

I cannot be certain how they feel, but I love this person and wish we could have a more satisfying relationship where we are more open with each other. While I am not entirely recasting this special character in my story, and am hopeful about assigning them another role in the future, for now, I decided it was time to focus on me.

Maybe you, too, have people in your life who are difficult or negative but remain there due to necessity. And maybe you feel that you can't or shouldn't entirely re-cast them. But you *can* control the access they have to your life and the amount of time they can be on stage.

Let's consider an example: being a theater director of a Broadway play.

Envision a scenario where you have been working hard, day in and day out, on a brand-new Broadway production. So far, you have been able to handle the hurdles and challenges, with the exception of one big setback: Sally. The show's producer—and your boss—strongly recommended that Sally be given a leading role even though she did not meet your standards of a star performer. As you quietly predicted, the overall success of the production is now suffering. Sally often shows up for rehearsals unprepared, she doesn't follow your direction on set, and she is disrespectful to other crew members. After several attempts to communicate with Sally, you notice that things still have not improved. If you could have it your way, you'd dismiss her immediately. The dilemma here, as you recently discovered, is that she is in a romantic relationship with the play's producer, and even though you feel sure that's why she was chosen for this role, you can't say that for certain. Now what? How will you handle this situation?

You may feel backed into a corner, but I believe that anyone can be recast if the thing at stake is remaining true to yourself. Begin by asking yourself if you are okay with what repercussions may follow your next decision. Are you willing to face the possibility of being fired yourself? Or will you stick your head in the sand and let Sally remain in her role? It is a tough choice, but ultimately, it is your call. Make a firm decision and stand by it. It's tough, but it's extremely important.

It's also important to understand that just because someone has a long-standing role in your past, it doesn't mean a guaranteed role moving forward. Relationships with difficult people are always a challenge, but when certain people are unable to meet your needs, a change in the relationship dynamic may be necessary. Strong communication and clearly stated expectations should always be at the forefront as you make any tough adjustment, because your cast mates may not be as understanding of your need for change.

Have you also reached a point in your life where you are tired of suffering? Are you ready to close the curtain on excessive drama? Will you allow yourself to be strong as you evaluate your supporting cast circles? Are you willing to accept the more challenging relationships and learn to work with them?

You can begin your evaluations by writing down all of your "main characters". Who are they and what are your expectations of them in your life right now? Next, place a star beside the names of people who are presenting more of a challenge to you. Finally, write down the steps that you would be willing to take in order to make those "starred" relationships stronger and more rewarding.

Take a closer look still. Could you possibly be a catalyst for someone else's suffering? Look at your main characters list again. Could any of those relationships be strained because of tension on both ends? Are you able to step outside your own comfort zone to be something better for someone who needs you? Who might that someone be? How will you begin to remedy that relationship?

Sometimes life feels like hard work. But, as with any good screenplay, it's the critical moments that have the power to change the course of our stories and make it a disaster or a box-office smash hit. This is your story, so fill it with a strong, supportive cast. Be grateful for all the people who have come and gone in your life, and for all the lessons they've taught you. Nurture the relationships that bring out the best in you. Be willing to let down your defenses and be open to seeing the things that could be changed. Have patience with yourself and with those around you. When you do these things, you will find that your story will flow more easily and teem with joy and fulfillment. When you love the ones you're with, you can truly create a story to remember.

17

"The more you praise and celebrate your life, the more there is in life to celebrate." —Oprah Winfrey

THE LITTLE MOMENTS

I am quite aware that many people out there have had to endure greater and more unimaginable challenges than mine, and I do not mean to discredit anyone's struggles. But one thing is for sure: it's how we rise up to meet life's challenges that defines our personal survive-and-thrive story.

Our stories are not only defined by the challenges we encounter, but also by our successes. It's our moments of free-spirited fun and embracing the familiar traditions of our life that should be highlighted, too, not just the hardships. Oftentimes, we become so preoccupied with our setbacks that we forget our triumphs and our instances of simply living life to the fullest, shoving them aside to collect dust. In this chapter, I encourage you to think about which life moments you are choosing to tell your story. Do you lean towards showcasing your joys or your troubles? Furthermore, consider which moments are the ones that help define the truly happy you.

To keep this activity more focused, think about specific

times from your childhood. Reflect on the times you truly felt free and just had fun. Start to jot down these memories. In doing so, the mental dust will start to clear and more joyful moments will be revealed. Later in the chapter, I will offer some ways to further jog your memory as you continue working towards allowing these good times to outshine the difficult ones.

Contrary to how it may have sounded in the previous chapter, not all the relationships in my life have been difficult. I, too, have many happy little moments from my childhood that could use some special attention.

I remember the many adventures I had at my babysitter's house during elementary school. There was the "haunted" red toolshed, the monstrous sledding hill we conquered in the winter, and the extra-long driveway that allowed for some pretty awesome Big Wheel stunts in the summer.

I remember my father's painstaking efforts to break my dual-finger sucking habit, and my very clever idea of offering him the wrong fingers when the sour-apple spray was in his hand. What a feeling of victory!

I remember the camping trips filled with hiking and sitting by the campfire. There were also the Sunday morning bike rides to the town bakery to enjoy fresh, warm bread topped with butter, cinnamon and sugar. I remember the tire swing up on the hill at Grandma's house and the heart-pounding excitement inspired by rounds of flashlight tag late in the evenings. I remember the never-ending board games I played with my very patient uncle.

I pestered boys, alternating between puppy-dog eyes and prank phone calls. I passed notes in class when I should have been paying attention and I played hooky at McDonald's. I remember band camp in the summer and football games and parades in the fall.

I remember who sat next to me on the bus in ninth grade and how our lives were forever changed when we became the unlikeliest of best friends. My tenth- grade World Cultures project produced some great laughs and paved the way for even more amazing memories. Things like a forbidden first kiss in the garage, a weekend of marathoning scary movies, and a silent climb through a window in the dark can't be forgotten.

I remember the true patience my father showed when I stalled out the manual transmission of his four-door Toyota Camry while learning to drive—not once, but twelve times before we even left our street!

I remember feeling beautiful in anything frilly, ruffled or shiny. I felt like a glamorous movie star when I put on my mother's perfume and long, silky nightgowns, watching the way the gown elegantly trailed behind me as I waltzed around the house.

I remember the triathlon I completed and how good it felt to turn around and see that, after barely making it up that last hill, I wasn't in last place after all. I can still hear my crazy Irish family members singing with glee at the annual Saint Patrick's Day party, where I'd help myself to all the special-occasion foods and treats. And I can't forget those times curled up into a hatchback trunk as we snuck into the local swimming hole.

It's amazing what a quick trip down memory lane can do for one's spirit! When I think about all these little moments, I am reminded again that life is full of joy and adventure; we just have to consciously choose to focus on these moments more often than the ones that cause discomfort.

Do you know what else is great about little moments like

these? It's that they are not only cherished by you, but they are often significant for others as well. My grandmother, for example, loves to tell everyone about the summer when she, my uncle and ten-year-old me drove from West Chester, Pennsylvania, all the way to Naples, Florida.

I know she enjoyed this trip just as much as I did just by the way she lights up when she tells her stories. She always smiles as she recalls the highlights of the trip. "We stopped for lunch somewhere, nothing fancy," she'll say, "and my granddaughter politely asked me what she could order. I told her that she could order anything that she wanted. And she looked at me with excitement and asked if she could order the shrimp!" She laughs just as hard now as she did that very day.

She'll also share the time that I slipped right out of the satin sheets on the sofa bed and landed on the floor. She'll chuckle as she recounts how, as a toddler, I was just the right height to walk under her kitchen table without hitting my head. And she still delights in the yummy strawberry milkshakes I prepared for her as a three-year-old running the makeshift shop that was her dishwasher.

I may not remember all of these things as vividly as she does, but it's significant how much of an impression these little moments have, even after all these years. These were moments that made her laugh, smile and just feel good inside. Thirty years later, they continue to bring her joy.

Now, look at the memories that you may have already written down. After reading about some of mine, can you remember any more special little moments of your own? If you are having trouble dusting things off, try some of these techniques to get things flowing.

- Consider these questions: What activities did you and your siblings enjoy regularly? Were there any family traditions or rituals that you particularly enjoyed while growing up? Who were your best friends in school and what do those friendships mean to you today?
- Pull out some of your old photo albums and use the photos to trigger your memory, again, taking note of those that stand out to you.
- Draw a map of your old city, town or neighborhood. You'll be surprised at what you start to recall.
- Call some of your friends and family and ask them to help you. Ask them to share some of the memories they have of you together.

You'll make someone else's day if you remind them of a laugh that you shared together. Make a mental note of a person in your life you could call or send a hand-written note to this week, and share that memory with them. Let them know that these moments continue to be special and important to you.

The more that you strive to actively create good memories, the more satisfying your life will be. Be proud of your stories, and make the choice to celebrate *your* little moments every day.

18

"Don't live the same year 75 times and call it a life." —
Robin Sharma, *The Monk Who Sold His Ferrari: A
Fable About Fulfilling Your Dreams & Reaching Your
Destiny*

THE DAYS YOU REMEMBER

Hopefully, you have started releasing some of those heavy anchors to your past and have freed up more space in your mind and heart for memorable moments. As you are working to become more mindful, you may have also found yourself slowing down to enjoy life's simple pleasures. In this chapter, I'd like to talk more about the importance of creating and recognizing the simple things in life.

Life is about a journey, it is not about a destination. Surely you have heard this quote before, but let's take a moment to focus on it. The epic-ness of our life journey should be measured by the moments that we create, the joy we feel at each given moment and the stories we have to tell. Our journey should be about more than just reaching a large goal like retirement, for example.

Many people see retirement as a marker for when their "life" and their "fun" will finally start. But by being so focused on that distant destination, they've missed out on the journey.

What I hope is for you to realize that you can make your story remarkable—right this very moment.

As you completed the memory exercise from the last chapter, it should have been apparent that there are people, places, things and even words that stay with us throughout our lives. Some of these are so inspiring and powerful that they completely change the direction of our life. I had mine changed once just from a simple phrase heard during an online TED Talk.

I had been hearing quite a few things about these TED Talks, but wasn't sure what they were all about. I imagined the larger-than-life, type-A personality jumping around theatrically on a ballroom stage as they tried to find the most innovative and unique ways to sell their message. While I might easily get caught up in the hype, within a few weeks, the momentum usually fizzles. Generally, that type of message marketing is not my cup of tea. Needless to say, I was quite skeptical about tuning in.

Luckily, my husband wasn't so closed-minded. He asked if he could play a TED Talk for me, and he asked if I would really listen to it. I agreed, and I have to say, its message was received loud and clear! After hearing Dustin Garis speak on "The Pursuit of a Memorable Life," I felt inspired. One of the points that hit home was when he said, "Life is not the number of days you live. It's the number of days you remember." With that simple phrase, I was not just inspired, I was overcome. I realized that, like him, I needed to change something about the way I was living my life. What's more, Mr. Garis succeeded in delivering his message by using only a few simple, yet effective, theatrical tools, such as a live graphic illustrator and a little goat who calmly pooped right on the stage. These things stood out because they were different. It's those small differences to our day, those subtle changes from the ordinary, that make things memorable. How could I not be moved by a cute, fearless goat?

It's been more than a year since I saw that talk, and my story has thankfully taken new, exciting and surprising turns. One surprising turn is that I am actively pursuing a life at sea. That's right. Remember when I mentioned that my husband and I were focused on creating a new story together? Our new story involves embarking on a family sailing adventure that we have dubbed *Onward Waves*. I will share more about this endeavor later in the book, but this huge life change is due, in large part, to Garis's philosophy. I truly have been working hard to make each day count and to find memorable moments to celebrate—or create—in more ways than one.

Now you might be asking, "How do I make today memorable when I feel so lousy?" You can find remarkable moments each day just by looking for them. I know it sounds cliché, but it really works.

Start by identifying something simple, yet memorable, that you experienced, saw, or felt today. Then think about something from yesterday, then from this week, then this month and this year. Special moments don't have to be big or expensive, like a vacation to Europe or getting a large raise. It can be something small like the bird hopping around outside your office window looking for a worm, or the new coworkers you met as you took the "long way" on the walk back to your office.

Let me share my example of recognizing the memorable moments in my own life.

Today: It's cold and windy here today. But the sun is

shining and I could feel its warmth as I got into my car. It made me smile. It made me thankful for simple pleasures.

Yesterday: After a challenging day at work, I was anxious to get home but needed to take my children to a doctor's appointment first. They were less than pleased with this plan and had no reservations voicing their complaints. This stretched the limits of my tolerance, and I asked them not to talk to me for a while as I was disappointed and needed time to process my thoughts. A bit later, after we returned home, I found a sticky note stuck to a leftover sandwich in the kitchen. It read, "Sorry Mommy. We are so spoiled. So eating this sandwich will make you feel better." This whole incident led to a really great family discussion that ended in laughter and farts. (Don't ask!)

This week: Just as my kids were about to arrive at the bus stop, I noticed that it was pouring rain. I contemplated jumping in the car and trying to meet them, but before I could, I saw the bright pink of my daughter's jacket rounding the far corner. Should I grab the umbrella and run to catch up with them? I decided not to do that. Instead, I opened the front door and started cheering her on as she made her way to the house. As soon as she saw me, she broke into a sprint. After finally reaching the house, smiling and a bit out of breath, she stated the obvious: that she had left her brother "in the dust." I again cheered and waved for my son, who had finally rounded the corner and started to run. Rain had soaked his hair and everything else, so, turning to face the sky, he took off his jacket and backpack and held them up in outstretched arms. He looked at me, and then up at the sky, with the biggest smile plastered across his innocent little face. This is what pure joy looks like. He completely immersed himself in the simple beauty of the world. He and I would have missed this beautiful moment if I decided to just pick them up in the car.

This month: I went to my first ever "Indie Authors Meetup." I was a little nervous, because I was a true newbie still in the beginning stages of writing my book. I thought I might not be "good enough" for a group like this. This couldn't have been further from the truth. Like I mentioned earlier about the importance of stepping outside your comfort zone, this turned out to be a great confidence booster for me. The people were amazing, and they had all different backgrounds and levels of writing experience. It felt good to share ideas and learn new things with a supportive and like-minded group. I can't wait for our next meeting.

This year: This year has been all about living and loving my life. It's been about spirituality and feeling connected with the universe. It's been about trying new things and working through layers of self-doubt. It's been about sailing and making our *Onward Waves* sailing dream happen, which, in turn, has also allowed me to re-focus and put some much-needed attention on my marriage.

It's been about raising my children to feel loved, happy, important and confident. I want them to be spiritually aware and curious. I want them to ask questions and to always be thankful and mindful of what they have, what they can do and what they can offer to others.

This year has been about finding the truly happy me.

What have *you* done today, yesterday, this week, this month, and this year that has been the most memorable? What dreams have you fulfilled? What small steps can you take today that might not only make a difference in your life, but maybe in someone else's as well? Make efforts to go about your day slowly and with intent—you might just be setting yourself up for an amazing transformation of your own.

What will you remember today?

19

"Friendship is the hardest thing in the world to explain. It's not something you learn in school. But if you haven't learned the meaning of friendship, you really haven't learned anything." —Muhammad Ali

BE A GOOD FRIEND

I've emphasized the importance of living in the moment and choosing to make these moments count. But how can we build connections with the people in our lives? First, we have to be a good friend. But what does it really mean to be a good friend, especially when we live in a society where social media rules?

Being a "friend" on social media sites these days is easy. All you need to do is simply "like" a photo or status, and you've earned your stripes. The other day I saw my niece scrolling through her Snapchat feed and hitting "like" so quickly that there was no way she could have processed each and every photo. It made me wonder if this was really all it takes. Can you really appreciate and respect your friends this way? Can we build empathy for other people in this way? Or are we all just looking to earn our friendship stripes?

I believe that being a good friend involves more than simply liking a status. We need to be the type of friend that we wish to have ourselves. It means going the extra mile and showing that you not only care about what is happening in your friend's life, but that you are also grateful to have them in yours. Equally important is that these feelings and actions are reciprocated. Otherwise, they may not make the final cut when you're doing your casting calls. True friendships shouldn't be hard work.

Do you find yourself saying or texting "I miss you!" or "We totally need to get together *soon!*" to your friends? After several weeks or months, do you find that the get-togethers still haven't happened?

If so, the next step is easy. You just need to follow through.

Put it on the calendar. Make the arrangements. Plan a daily or weekly phone call. Send snail mail or a surprise care package. Whatever it takes to make the "Get together soon" text turn into "Thank you for thinking of me!" or "So great to see you! Can't wait for next time!" text. Just this year, my husband and I have made a resolution to call or send a personal note to all of our friends and family on Facebook. I hope that by doing this, I will not only show them that they are important to me, but that I will truly begin the process of making the kind of close personal connections we all need. What more might come from doing this, I'll have to wait and see. Try it for yourself and let me know how it turned out for you.

As easy as "being a good friend" sounds, I know from experience that it can often be difficult to trust someone. Even a friend. Sometimes we work so hard trying to paint a perfect picture of our life that we forget that our true friends don't care how perfect or imperfect we are. For me, one of the hardest parts of my journey was reaching out and asking my friends and family for help. There were many reasons why I felt that I should deal with my pain alone. I was scared to let my guard down and feel defenseless; I was scared that my friends or family would not support me in the way I expected; I didn't want to seem stupid; I didn't want people to see anything but a masterpiece.

But my biggest reason for not asking a friend for help? I was embarrassed. Asking for anything made me feel weak and vulnerable, just like laughing. It made me feel ashamed, like I had done something wrong.

But none of these reasons were acceptable excuses for continuing to silently suffer.

What would you say or do for a friend if you knew they needed help but were too ashamed to ask? Wouldn't you encourage them to talk to you? Wouldn't you comfort them and try to ease their concerns? Wouldn't you go out of your way, even just a little, to make them feel secure? I know I would. How is it, then, that when the tables are turned, we can be so blind and so resistant to our own needs?

One thing that comes to mind when I think of having solid, true friendships in life is the classic song "Lean on Me" by Bill Withers. It may seem silly initially, but when you consider the lyrics, they really offer such an honest message. I am sure you have heard this song before, and it may even be on your playlist of positive, empowering songs. But feel free to reacquaint yourself with it by listening to it on your music app.

Go ahead—I'll wait.

Did you feel that? The energy and emotion that built up as you listened? The message is clear. We all need a friend to call on during our times of need, and we should also *be* the friend that others can call on. We need to swallow our pride, push aside our ego, and ask for what we need. We must feel safe when it comes to showing our weaknesses, and have faith that others will help build us back up. Sometimes learning to ask for help, and then accepting it, is a hard thing to do. But the more you fill your support circles with true friends and caring family, the easier it will be.

Here is another thing that I feel is an important part of being a good friend—giving hugs. For all the huggers out there this is good news, but for many people who feel intimidated by the perceived intimacy of hugs, this can be nerve-racking. Some people are "half huggers" and some are "bear huggers." Half huggers give hugs that include things like a moment of hesitation as you both go to the same side and an awkward chuckle as you switch directions, all followed by a slight lean-in and small pats on the back. The bear huggers give big, strong hugs. They are the ones who stretch their arms out wide to completely engulf the other person.

Where do you fall on the hugging scale? While most of us fall somewhere in between, one study done at Carnegie Mellon University suggested that a hug lasting longer than twenty seconds offers the best benefits. That means just as you, the "hugger" feels the "huggee" starting to pull away, you should hold on a just a little tighter and a little bit longer. It might cause some awkwardness at first, but just hold on! They will soon begin to relax and hug back, as their expectations of a quick, meaningless hug are diminished. They (and you) will remember this hug for sure. Hugs make us feel good, comfortable and safe. Go ahead and try it! Hug like you mean it!

Hugging can also be so much more than just an awkward hello or goodbye. In an article entitled "10 Reasons Why We Need at Least 8 Hugs a Day" written by Marcus Julian

Felicetti on the website MindBodyGreen, he summed up some of the great healing benefits of hugging. A few of my favorite points from his article were that just by giving and receiving good hugs, we increase our own sense of trust, safety, self-esteem and self-love. Hugs soothe aches and pains by releasing tension and increasing circulation through our body. Additionally, they trigger the production of neurochemicals such as serotonin and oxytocin, helping to heal feelings of loneliness and anger while also working to elevate our mood and create feelings of happiness.

So, the next time an opportunity arises to offer up a good hug, hold on to that person just a while longer. When you feel them start to pull away, keep holding on! There are too many positive reasons to not enjoy a good hugging session.

In the end, being a good friend shouldn't be hard work. Nurture the relationships in your life that work. Identify the friends with whom you want to fulfill the "Let's get together!" promise and make it happen. And when you see them, go in for a nice big hug for good measure.

20

"The single biggest problem in communication is the illusion that it has taken place." —George Bernard Shaw

A VOICE FOR HAPPINESS

Isn't it amazing the power words can have? Whether written or spoken, words impact our lives in so many ways. They can evoke a wide range of feelings, thoughts and emotions. They can be used to build us up or even tear us down.

There are thousands of books written about the power of words, and probably hundreds more on specific ways to build solid communication skills. These books promise to show you how to formulate statements in the most efficient and effective way possible. They often guarantee to make you a more impactful leader, a better parent, or a more engaged and caring spouse.

What they have in common is that they all say that our words have to be direct, honest and pure; you have to say what you mean and mean what you say. And being a successful communicator has to start with you speaking and thinking kind thoughts about yourself first.

During a team-building seminar a few years ago,

something the speaker said stuck with me. (And that's right—years later I'm chalking this up as another "ah-ha" moment).

He said: *"Unstated expectations lead to guaranteed resentments."*

Wow! I was blown away by the truth this statement represented in both my professional and my personal lives. I was the queen of unstated expectations, with years of practice under my belt. My expectations were not only silent, they were unreasonably high as well. And as many of them would go unmet, they made me feel frustrated and angry. When the years passed and my communication skills remained subpar, I got angrier and more resentful of the people close to me. *I was living my life anticipating disappointments.* What good could possibly come of that?

As my healing journey progressed, I began to notice how much negativity I created through words left unspoken. They influenced my mood in more ways than I'd like to admit. With trouble brewing in my marriage, I came back to, *"Unstated expectations lead to guaranteed resentments."* I knew that I needed to not only re-shape my thoughts, but also learn to verbalize them more effectively.

Let's look at another example of self-sabotaging behavior. Here, again, you'll see how I was holding myself captive by thinking only the worst.

Prior to my healing journey, I was not very loving or accepting of myself; I wasn't confident in who I was because I didn't *know* who I was. As I mentioned, I was always trying to force myself into the molds of the perfect woman, daughter, wife and mother I thought I should be. I was a chameleon, adapting and changing to fit my environment. I had suppressed the real "me" for so long that I wouldn't have even recognized myself if we were sitting face to face. This is not a sustainable state of being, and it's especially challenging in a marriage.

My husband, in my opinion, is a very wise and uncomplicated soul. On a regular basis, he shows his true colors of thoughtfulness, patience and a willingness to go the extra mile for someone in need. He is also ambitious, hardworking and talented – a true MacGyver type. With an easy-going, positive attitude and welcoming smile, he can make friends with just about everyone he meets. He laughs a lot and, though sometimes corny, he has a great sense of humor, too. My husband is not afraid of failure and will face defeat admirably, with a reflective and calm demeanor before setting off to try again. He is nonjudgmental, loyal and forgiving. He is a voice of reason, a go-getter, and an adventurer. He is so many things that I thought I should be—and wasn't.

I assumed that I brought nothing comparable to the table. Unknowingly, I had made our marriage and parenting into a *competition*. Me against him. I always tried to have the upper hand. I felt that I had to question and out-do his every move. Instead of us working together, united as a loving, supportive team, I rallied to be victorious all on my own. In allowing myself to keep this pessimistic attitude, I began to resent my husband. I was angry at the man with all those admirable and desirable qualities that I had fallen in love with so many years ago. Really, I was jealous. Jealous that he was able to be true to himself and he did not have to be a chameleon like me.

I must have made his job as a husband very hard. He had to deal with a lot of highs and lows of my personality. He had to learn to make sense of my nonsense. There were many times, I am sure, that I unintentionally forced him to choose.

Subconsciously, he had to choose between letting go or learning to love someone who couldn't always love him the way that he desired and deserved. I also put a lot of pressure on him to make me happy, like it was his responsibility.

He often attempted to shed some light on my many misconceptions. He tried to show me that he alone could not fix what I thought was broken within myself or make me feel happy and satisfied with my life. He tried to explain how unfair I was being, especially to myself, when I chose to put my sense of self-worth and happiness in the hands of others. Yet I did not believe his words and I continued on, still silently expecting him to perform miracles.

Eventually, I began to realize that it was not anyone else's responsibility to make me happy. It was up to me and me alone. I was the only one who could make *me* happy. I was the one who needed to see the toxicity I was creating by choosing to remain silent and live in a world full of unstated expectations. Where was my positive, affirming voice? Couldn't I see the damage I was causing? Couldn't I see how fragile I became when I didn't trust or love myself first? Or how susceptible I was to self-destruction when I chose to think I was forever broken?

I forced myself to really open my eyes and acknowledge all of those pitfalls for what they were. Then, I needed to gather the strength and the willpower to change them. Most importantly, if I really wanted to start moving forward towards change, I had to make the choice to love myself. I needed that true sense of self-love if I wanted my wounds to heal and my true happiness to be felt. My survival of self, and my marriage, depended on this.

While it may be hard at first, truly loving who you are and

changing that voice in your head to be positive and loving will begin paving your way towards healing and joy. Think back to the statement, "Unstated expectations lead to guaranteed resentments." What does this mean to you and how does it apply to your life right now? In what ways could you work to build up your own self-confidence and self-love? A good place to start is to commit to being open and honest with yourself and within your relationships. Equally important is that you feel strong and confident in communicating your expectations. Be courageous enough to voice your opinions, thoughts, concerns and ideas. Change the voice in your head. Be the positive voice of happiness to yourself and to others. Keep powering forward. It is only when we begin speaking out loud and quieting the negative chatter in our minds that our true voices will be heard.

21

"Be happy. It's one way of being wise." —Sidonie
Gabrielle Colette

UNEXPECTED WISDOM FROM UNEXPECTED PLACES

Sometimes, you discover clues to a happier you in the most unexpected places. If you had to guess, what age group would you think lives the most carefree life? Which age group do you think can offer you the most practical advice?

Did you guess, perhaps, the older generation? I bet that's what most people would say, however, I would argue that it's a tie between children under thirteen and adults over sixty-five. Both of these groups have a unique vantage point and can offer a wealth of wisdom and knowledge if we take the time to ask them. And then listen to them. And then reflect on what we have heard.

As I was writing this book and becoming more mindful of what was going on in my own life, I wondered if I could learn something about personal happiness from one of these groups. I went searching for a reputable source, and I didn't have to look very far. I had a pretty wise and unique individual right in the next room.

My seven-year-old daughter is the epitome of what I call a

"Three S" personality. She is smart, sweet and sassy. She was born on her predicted due date and has kept me on my toes ever since. She once told me that *she chose me* as her parent instead of it being all my and her father's doing—a belief with which I have come to wholeheartedly agree. My daughter has taught me more lessons than I would have ever thought possible, the main one being patience. She is bold, brave and fearless, always pushing the limits or climbing to the highest part of the tree. She is competitive and has a natural athletic ability that helps her keep up with her older brother or reach a finish line first. Her strong and vibrant personality often leaves me laughing hysterically or with several new gray hairs. She is inquisitive and knows what she wants—even if it's often the opposite of what I think she needs. Nevertheless, her counterpoints in a disagreement have left me speechless on several occasions. Without a doubt, she is wise beyond her years.

My husband and I do our best to encourage a strong sense of inner reflection and open-mindedness with both of our children. We also try to incorporate and introduce tools and techniques such as yoga, meditation and prayer into their daily routines. While both of my children understand the benefits of whole-body wellness, my daughter has a real knack for insightful and descriptive language. So it made sense, then, that I should inquire how she thought one should deal with their difficult feelings, thoughts or emotions. The following two mental exercises are courtesy of my daughter, after I asked her what she does to lift her spirits when she feels upset or troubled.

Look Out the Window (At Night)

"I look out the window at night," she said. "I look at our lights and the other people's lights and the trees. Pretend it's an airport runway."

She uses that runway to take off on a guided meditation, leaving all of her difficult emotions behind. In her imagination, she flies around admiring the Earth's beauty, visiting any place in the world and playing with all the cute and cuddly animals that she wants. Being in charge of this guided meditation, she can visualize anything that makes her happy.

From her window, she sees the soft glow of streetlights, the swaying of trees, and the gentle light of the stars and the moon. When she is ready, and she feels like the storm inside her has passed, she'll make her landing, noticing her soft breath on the window pane. She feels calm and peaceful. There are no more loud noises, no more troubling emotions. Just the gentle quiet of her world within and around her.

Her exercise is a simple, yet powerful, one. By choosing to board that imaginary airplane, you are essentially giving yourself permission to leave all your mental negativity behind. That's just what you need to do in order to begin releasing your worries. And as you continue the exercise, looking outside at night, when the world is at its most quiet and serene, you will feel calmer and more relaxed. Life is full of hurried days, and it's easy to forget that we are just a tiny speck in this grand universe. By reflecting on this simple beauty, we surely can breathe a little deeper and smile a little wider.

While my daughter suggests doing this at night, I'm quite certain that it will work just as well in the daytime. So, clear your runway for departure, leave your worries at the gate and begin to awaken some inner sunshine of your own.

The Beauty of Black

Here is another easy and creative way to deal with a troubled or overactive mind, especially when we have those obsessive thoughts that just won't stop. My daughter suggests that you can just "paint your mind black."

In this simple exercise, you become a master artist. But this time we are not going to be painting pictures of what we want the world to see; instead, we are closing our eyes and envisioning painting our thoughts and concerns away. You can choose whatever size paintbrush you want—small and fine-bristled or large and wide—depending on just how big and consuming your thoughts are.

Once you have a chosen brush, dip it in elegant black paint. Then, envision each brush stroke as it makes its way across the canvas of your mind. Back and forth, each line absorbing the busyness and clutter of your thoughts. Anytime a negative thought tries to sneak back into your mind, just add more brush strokes right over top of it. If it still lingers, visualize the thought in its written form, and slowly pull it out and away from you like a fine hair and drop it into your mental garbage can. Or you can imagine its letters and words falling down haphazardly, like in a cartoon, only to be absorbed into the lacquer of your masterpiece. Take a few deep breaths and continue painting your masterpiece until the anxiety has subsided and you feel in control again. You have now created a sophisticated blackness that protects you, easing you into a relaxing, quiet, safe space. You should feel renewed and calm.

This is the beauty of black.

As you can see, some of the most insightful, and practical, advice can come from the most unlikely of places. Can you identify a person in your life, younger than thirteen or older than sixty-five, that you'd like to ask advice from? Ask how they might go about lifting their spirits when feeling upset or troubled. You may be pleasantly surprised at what they have to say.

So, let this chapter serve as a reminder to be open to *inquiring* and *acquiring* wisdom from some unexpected places.

22

"Time is a created thing. To say 'I don't have time,' is like saying 'I don't want to.'" —Lao Tzu

THE ISLAND TIME APPROACH

I used to set some pretty hard deadlines for myself.

I am not talking about the kind of deadlines you have at work, like the analysis of the company's upcoming merger that must be done and presented tomorrow to the CEOs and CFOs and ABCs and the Who's Who of mega-important people. Nope. That's baby stuff compared to my deadlines. My hard deadlines were way more important than that—or, at least, they seemed that way to me. These deadlines were things that I felt *had* to be done by a certain time.

I know you are probably thinking that everyone has these types of hurdles, right? Everyone has things for which they are accountable. To a certain extent, you are correct. But let me introduce you to a hard deadline I set that caused nothing but trouble.

The deadline of the eight-o'clock bedtime.

Please don't laugh. It's true. For a long time, I had the unstated expectation (remember those?) that when the clock struck eight, my children would be in bed, eyes closed and ready to sleep like good little robots. Beep, beep.

But I have human children, not robots. They weren't programmable—nor were they attuned to my silent expectations—and thus they were hardly ever ready for bed by the time the clock struck eight. My patience meter was already low, and with every second that ticked on, it would get lower. As pre-bedtime chores were left undone, or one of my children made a request or asked yet another seemingly unanswerable question about life, my frustration would mount.

I yelled, I chided, and I am sure my face expressed every ounce of anger and annoyance that I was feeling. And all of this because of what? Because a little black pointer was moving around an enclosed circle? Because I assigned meaning to the numbers on that circle? Yes to both of those. But it was also because *I was selfish.* It might be excusable to act this way once or twice, here or there. But all the time? I was not being fair to my children at all.

As I was progressing in my self-discovery, I began to see how my actions during our nightly routine were causing some major consequences.

- I was robbing my children of a quiet and relaxed end of their day, something they deserved.
- I was giving them the impression that I did not have time for them because my needs were more important than theirs.
- We were missing opportunities to share and create memorable moments.
- I was sending incredibly negative messages with

my scowls and impatience, suggesting that asking questions or being curious was a nuisance and something to be discouraged.

All of this was because it was eight o'clock and I was tired. By the time I finally got into my own bed, I felt remorseful and ashamed. I knew that I had to figure out a way to ease up on these self-imposed deadlines. I did not want my children to have negative memories of what should be a time of peace and happiness; more importantly, I didn't want them to end their day feeling unloved.

Hence, I came up with something I like to call "the island time approach." The island time approach is more a way of life than an answer to a single problem, but it's quite helpful when dealing with many of the absurd expectations that we seem to hold for ourselves, and often of others, too.

In order to start practicing this approach, just imagine that you are on an endless vacation on a tropical island. When you are on this vacation, you're on island time. Everything on island time is carefree, moving nice and slow. The weather is warm with a salty breeze, and you can feel the sand between your toes as you watch waves crash along the shore from a large Adirondack chair. There are no clocks to be seen. Tasks and jobs on the island get done when they get done. You are not concerned with things that happened yesterday, and you are not consumed by thoughts of what tomorrow might bring. You are fully engaged in your present moment and accepting of its ebb and flow.

This sounds simple, and it should be. But living on island

time takes a little getting used to. You may need to take a few deep breaths or close your eyes to re-focus your attention on the present moment and help reorganize your thoughts. It's important to realize that we cannot draw lines in the sand and expect the ocean to comply. If we are overly focused on those lines, and on not letting them get washed away, we will certainly miss out on enjoying the beauty of what's right there in front of us. And if we aren't careful, we might be robbing others of that beauty, too!

Is there an area in *your* life that might benefit from the perspective of "the island time approach?" Once you get the hang of it, you'll be able to relax, let go, and enjoy living your life on island time.

23

"Do not go where the path may lead; go instead where there is no path and leave a trail." —Ralph Waldo Emerson

THE RALLY FOR CHILDHOOD DRIVE

D o you have a strong sense of self-reliance? If you do, you likely trust yourself and feel confident in your own efforts and abilities. Many adults struggle with these things, including myself, yet it often seems that very young children are brimming with self-confidence. Why is that? I saw a meme the other day featuring a baby of about twelve months old. The caption read: "When a child learns to walk and falls down fifty times, he never thinks to himself: 'Maybe this isn't for me?'"

There is a reason why children don't give up—they haven't yet been taught to doubt themselves. This is another reason why they can be such an excellent source of inspiration, as they haven't been taught the difference between believing in themselves and giving up. They instinctively keep trying until they succeed at changing, growing, and learning in order to overcome obstacle after obstacle.

If we were lucky at this age, we already had a supporting cast, clapping and cheering us on. They celebrated our victories, but they also celebrated our failures, as each one meant we were taking a step towards learned success. It was a life of constant encouragement and praise, inspiring us to press on.

Sadly, many of us can't remember our own milestone moments. We can't remember our first steps, our first time going without a diaper or the first time we got dressed all by ourselves. We can't remember reciting our ABCs, learning to tie our own shoes, or mastering riding our bike without training wheels. But we do know that, during moments like those, we felt proud of ourselves, loving the rush of excitement and the feeling of doing something great. We smiled, laughed and probably even clapped for ourselves.

What if our life was like that now? What if we, as adults, retained that childhood drive? That strong sense of self-confidence and self-love? Of pushing ourselves to succeed in the big things and the little things? What happened to not blaming ourselves and not giving up? Why do we now see failures as disappointments instead of as stepping stones towards learned success? Who, and where, are our supportive teams, cheering and helping us along our way?

You are in charge of something incredible: the story of your life. Many people take this for granted—often we hesitate to reevaluate the meaning of our lives until a great tragedy occurs, one that forces us to go back to the beginning, to dig down and find true, instinctive strength. It is usually moments like this when we realize that we have the choice to make our life as great—or as insufferable—as we want it to be.

From the very beginning, from the moment you were born and first opened your eyes, *that* was when you decided to live. Make the choice to open your eyes again. See the beauty that surrounds you and know that you can create an amazing life story each moment, each hour, and each day. Are you ready to act like a kid again? If so, begin by making the choice to rally for a stronger, more steadfast you. It's your childhood drive that can provide a little extra fuel to your inner spark, helping propel you even more towards the truly happy you.

24

"Your task is not to seek for love, but merely to seek and find all the barriers within yourself that you have built against it." —Jalaluddin Rumi

FREE YOURSELF FROM YOURSELF

For the majority of my childhood, there was a prominent figure in my life who treated me unfairly, and who, it seemed to me, was always quick to criticize and slow to praise. Whether it was to make passive-aggressive comments about the way I dressed, how I wore my makeup, or even towards the simplest of things I said or did, my sense-of-self really took a beating. This person's condescending words and tones, disappointed glances, and spiteful behaviors are the memories that stand out to me the most. I never felt good enough. The negative physical actions—which at times included things like kicking, grabbing my arm, and pulling my hair—and the lack of nurturing behaviors, made me feel unloved, ugly and insecure, not to mention sad and confused. How is a young child, let alone a grown adult, supposed to react to such frequent acts of disapproval? How can a young person grow into their own unique identity if they don't first know how to believe in themselves?

There are many reasons why people treat one another

with disrespect. When people act out in hurtful ways, they themselves are not at peace. They are often holding on to past anger and resentments that are now beyond their control. They allow those things to influence them in very powerful and often negative ways.

At a very early age, I began to find ways to manipulate my environment in order to find solace. One way was to adhere to the phrase "out of sight, out of mind." I figured that if I could just find a way to be as invisible as possible, then I would be okay. I began to devise ways to avoid the person who was hurting me. For example, if I was upstairs getting ready for school and he/she was downstairs, I would begin my espionage, walking halfway down the stairs to look into the glass of one of the picture frames hanging along the staircase wall. Through its reflection of the living room, I could see if anyone was there before they could even see my feet. If it was empty, I would quietly step down one or two more steps so I could use another picture to peer into the kitchen. If the coast was clear, I would make a beeline to the bathroom or just head out to the bus stop. While it's pretty difficult for a hearing-impaired person to be sneaky, I found that staying out of sight kept me out of the line of fire.

When I couldn't avoid being seen, I would do everything I could to try to please people. I learned that when people are in a good mood, they are less likely to find fault in the things around them. As I got older, I continued making huge efforts to say and do the right thing at all times and at all costs. This meant that many times I would compromise my own morals. In my mind, if people were happy with me, that meant they appreciated me. And if I could get them to appreciate me, then they would love me—or like me, or need me, or value me, or desire me. It varied depending on whether the person I was trying to please was a parent, a friend, a boyfriend, a teacher or a stranger, but all of those interactions expressed the same longing to feel important. Again, I was living my life in search of an identity that would please everyone—except me.

Being a chronic people-pleaser can have several long-term side effects. Low self-esteem, poor coping skills and many other self-defeating patterns of behavior can take root. When you crave approval and validation in such an addictive way, you will seek it out any way that you can. Inadvertently, this puts a tremendous amount of value on how other people think, feel and act, diminishing the importance of your own thoughts, feelings, wants and needs. Ultimately, overall dissatisfaction prevails.

If you are feeling dissatisfied, it's easy to fall into a vicious cycle of constant complaining. This happened to me, and while sometimes I would voice my complaints, mostly they just stayed in my head and clogged it up with negative chatter. This constant complaining gave me a toddler complex that haunted me for years with its refrains of "Why me?" and "It's not fair!" For example:

"Why do I have a hearing disability? It's not fair!"

"Why was my past like that? It's not fair!"

"Why can't I have that money, success, beauty, *et cetera* that they have? It's not fair!"

I acted like a child in so many ways. I would pout, whine and give others the silent treatment if I didn't get my way. I was stubborn (my excuse was that I am a Taurus), as well as feisty and temperamental (my excuse was that I am a redhead). I trained myself to expect the worst, my glass always half-empty.

Over the years, my anger and resentment just continued to bubble up like a quiet volcano. When that volcano finally erupted, I was faced with my biggest challenge yet. How was I supposed to escape all the mental and emotional abuse that I was suffering from if the abuser was *me*?

Are you guilty of this type of self-abuse? Do you long to feel loved and accepted by everyone? Do you find that you complain a lot about things that are beyond your control? Are you using your past experiences as a crutch? Are you looking to build self-love and self-acceptance in all the wrong ways and in all the wrong places? If any of these statements hold true for you, begin a path towards healing by *freeing yourself from yourself*.

Your old defensive mechanisms are no longer needed. I, for one, don't need to check for reflections in picture frames anymore, and I don't want to be out of sight, out of mind either. You shouldn't be a hostage to things like that anymore. Our ego, that little voice in our heads, is like a narrator for our life story, and although it may be hard to believe, we *are* in charge of that narration.

Our egoistic thoughts are just that, thoughts. The ego goes about inserting narrative thoughts into our daily life. Think of it like one of those choose-your-own-adventure books, one where in addition to constantly making decisions, we can also choose how our narrator behaves. We can choose to let that voice be loud or soft, demeaning or encouraging, and even choose to turn it on or off. The most important thing to realize is that that voice does not need to control your story.

Let's say, for example, you are feeling downcast. If your ego is turned up to full volume, it may be trying to turn that simple feeling of sadness into an all-out crisis. However, you have the ability to choose which page in your adventure novel to turn to next. Will you let that downcast feeling spiral into full-on misery, staying inside alone with the shades drawn and covers over your head? Will you choose to complain and skip out on your social functions?

Or will you choose to simply acknowledge your feeling of sadness, allowing yourself to experience that emotion for a short time before offering yourself comfort and compassion? You might then choose to take off your shoes and walk around the park, feeling the grass beneath your feet and the sunshine on your face. As you begin to feel happier, you could put a smile on your face and even offer one to your ego. Then, stretch your arms up to the sky, fingers far apart, take a deep breath, and say, "Thank you! Here I am!"

Work on choosing the best adventure for each moment. Take a more active role in how your story goes. Continue working on loving yourself and becoming the person you want to be.

What are you waiting for? Take control of your inner narration and set yourself free.

25

"If you are going through hell, keep going." —Sir Winston Churchill

ADVICE: IF YOU GIVE IT, LIVE IT

In my line of work, I don't just "clean teeth." I am an oral health therapist who dabbles in a variety of other specialties such as teacher, friend, cheerleader, comedian, confidante, cancer screener, advocate for natural or herbal remedies, and—my favorite—personal therapist. The fact that I am inquisitive helps me get right to the heart of many of my patients' stresses, concerns and questions, many of which play an indirect, and sometimes direct, role in their oral health. Yes, I am appreciated by many of my patients for so much more than just "cleaning their teeth" and by offering them an ear, I have found that I have a wealth of creative and unique advice to offer.

At some point during my journey, I woke up to the fact that I couldn't expect the great advice I shelled out to my patients to help if I didn't follow that advice myself.

I can't say it enough: loving and accepting yourself is a huge part of living a happy and fulfilled life. If you are still trying to figure out how to do that, taking and trusting your own advice is usually a great starting point. Here are a few tidbits that I've given others and am working to incorporate into my own life.

- Stop caring about what other people are thinking about you. Better yet, stop thinking that other people *are* thinking about you.
- Time is irrelevant. This moment right now is all we need to focus on.
- Keep a thesaurus handy. Fancy words will make you feel ~~good and smart~~ poised and scintillating.
- Don't put off for tomorrow what you can do today. Procrastination is not your friend. (Yeah, I'm working on that one).
- Be vulnerable. We grow the most during times of greatest uncertainty.
- Be a positive example. Act in ways that you would want others to act. With dignity, integrity, kindness, respect and compassion.
- Life is not a competition. Do not succumb to the lure of trying to out-do everyone else. That super fancy character birthday party with pony rides for your coworker's two-year-old? That does not have to be a "challenge accepted" scenario.
- Say "I love you," "I'm sorry," "You're right, I'm wrong," and "Thank you" when you mean it. Say "yes" when you want to do something and "no" when you don't.
- It's okay to say "I don't know" if you don't understand or are unsure. But it's not okay if you don't try to understand or try to be more aware.

- When you find something that allows more joy into your life, stick with it. It may not always work out in the end, but it will certainly open doors along the way that can help you learn more about yourself.
- Be brave enough to make your own decisions, even if they seem too scary or difficult. Making decisions on your own allows you to feel stronger and gives you traction that helps you become "un-stuck." Be aware that many times the decisions that we think we need to make will seem dangerous, crazy or unsupported by others. This is the moment when you remind yourself that you are no longer a people-pleaser. You are a self-pleaser.
- Remember that you are living your life for you, not for anyone else. When you are happy, then you can help make others happy, too.
- Do not compare your life to someone else's. We all have our own unique journey to live and story to create.
- Life is better when you decide to take that trip, eat that slice of cake, wear those shoes...or, of course, sail that boat!
- Always trust your gut.

Here's another idea you might like to try: create a mission statement for your life, just like a successful company does in order to remind the world what it stands for. This can help you stay focused on your goals and on your journey. You can always go back and adjust your statement as needed. Take care not to make it about proving others wrong. Use it to prove to yourself that you will succeed in living a happy, fulfilled life.

Hopefully, some of these thoughts and ideas resonate with you and inspire you to keep moving forward. If you are feeling unhappy with yourself, don't wait for someone, or something, to fix that. You need to find a way for *you* to love you. Prove to yourself that you are worthy of living an amazing life, and then you will have the strength, wisdom and courage to make that a reality.

Now, take my advice—and follow yours.

26

"Life is what happens to you while you're busy making other plans." —John Lennon

TURN OFF AND TUNE IN

It's been a long time since the phrase "I'm bored" actually meant something. I feel like we have lost the ability to be bored. These days we have smartphones, video games, iPads, iPods and even virtual reality glasses! We have everything we need to keep our minds busy right at our fingertips. In fact, if anything, our problem is overstimulation.

In this chapter, I ask that you spend a few moments reflecting on the amount of time that you spend "zoning out." Think about the amount of time you spend on your phone while working, riding the subway home, waiting to eat, or while "watching" your kids play.

I'll admit, I used to zone out a lot. Whether it was Facebook, YouTube or Pinterest, I could get lost for hours, just scrolling. I felt a sense of connection to family, friends and even complete strangers. I held the belief that by "liking" pictures, posts and status updates, I was truly connecting with these people. I felt like we were real-time BFFs.

One day, I sent a private message to one of my hundreds of

BFFs, a friend whom I had not actually seen or spoken with for many years. In my message, I offered kind and reassuring words as it appeared she was going through a difficult marital separation.

I remember being a little shocked by what she wrote back. She responded by saying thank you and that she really appreciated my reaching out. She wrote that not many people had reached out to her, or even seemed to notice the struggles she was going through. She ended her response by saying that she was very thankful to me for being "such a good friend."

A good friend? Why was I shocked by this? This was what I wanted to hear, wasn't it? While I'm glad that I was able to provide comfort, where were her *real* BFFs when she needed them? This incident made me ask myself: what was I really getting from my addiction to my social media accounts?

During my journey, I made a tough decision to disconnect from my social media for a whole year. In the beginning, I missed all the instant notification alerts and gossip. Those early weeks were painful. I felt a huge sense of loss and abandonment—significant emotions given that all I had stopped doing was scrolling through hundreds of photos, pins and status updates. I realized that I was using my social media accounts to make me feel meaningful; I was relying on thumbs-ups for validation, not to mention that I thrived on drama, negativity and judging the lives of strangers. It was a real wake-up call, for sure.

Now that you've estimated the amount of time you spend on your own accounts, here's the next challenge. I challenge you to "turn off" and instead allow yourself to be fully present. Can you turn off and tune in? What new connections could you make within yourself and with others now that you have some extra time on your hands? How much stronger mentally and emotionally do you think you could be with a quieter and more conscious mind? What people in your life could benefit from seeing you more frequently, speaking with you more often or learning from you?

The take-home message here: Your social networks are not giving you what you think they are. So, challenge yourself to make a different choice. Turn off the electronics and immerse yourself in the most important moment you have: this one. Talk to strangers, work in the garden, listen to a child tell you stories about their day. Let yourself be bored. Tap into your inner child and get creative with your time—color, draw, go roller skating. You just might discover something special that you never even knew you were looking for!

27

"If you have good thoughts, they will shine out of your face like sunbeams and you will always look lovely."
—Roald Dahl

CAPTURE YOURSELF UNAWARE

Electronic technology has become abundant, and as I mentioned in the last chapter, it can also be quite taxing. While I know that I just challenged you to turn off the electronics, you will need them for this next activity. I promise it's for a good purpose. This is a photography and video challenge, so feel free to use what you've got.

Let me first tell you how the idea for this came about. A few months ago, I recorded myself on video during a sailing class that I was participating in. Once I viewed this video, it got me thinking how most people, including myself, tend to modify their behavior when they are aware of being observed by outsiders. It's as if we have a "dual persona" of sorts. We always want strangers to see the "best" side of our personalities. Meanwhile, we tend to let down our guard, be vulnerable and show our "worst" side around those to whom we are closest. Unfortunately, that means we might not always treat our loved ones as respectfully as we should. Could you say that you argue the same way with your boss as you do with your significant other? Do you reprimand your children the same way you would someone else's child? Do you feel comfortable wearing a "lazy Sunday" outfit—and attitude—to the office on a Tuesday?

Before I assign your challenge, let me share how my sailing video, as well as two other examples, helped further my curiosity of this "dual persona" concept.

The first example highlights just how perceptive children can be in regards to the people and the personalities around them. My daughter, then a kindergartener, would often complain that her teacher was mean. I was boggled, as her teacher seemed nothing short of pleasant and kind whenever I saw her. I assumed that my daughter was exaggerating and shared my impressions with her. My daughter replied, "She always smiles and is nice when parents are there. But as soon as you leave, she is back to being angry and yelling at us."

I realized that there wasn't much I could say; my daughter is entitled to her opinion, and what's more, she had more experience to form that opinion. To give the teacher some credit, I tried to explain that being a teacher is a lot of hard work. I went on to point out that the teacher is responsible for many children each day. I asked my daughter to step into her teacher's shoes and consider just how challenging the job can be. While my daughter wasn't easily convinced, this moment taught me to be more mindful and respectful of my children's (and others') thoughts and opinions. Their observations do matter and should count for something.

The second example is a coach from my son's sports team. During the season, I witnessed frustrated sighs, heavy words and disappointed glances and comments, even to his own children.

I was confused. My first impression of him had been good. He smiled and joked at our parent meeting. He seemed very knowledgeable and enthusiastic for the season ahead. So, was my initial judgment wrong?

I don't think so. What I do think is that he was just unaware of his off-camera persona. Meaning, the messages and visuals that he was sending when he wasn't focused on wowing the crowd were different than when he was trying to impress a group of parents. After all, don't we all "play nice" for the cameras when we know we are being observed?

After that revelation, I began thinking more about how I looked when I was "off camera." With that unscripted video from the sailing class that I mentioned earlier, I got my answer. I was taking a sailboat docking course on the Chesapeake Bay and I had hooked up my Go-Pro camera to record some of the techniques I was learning. Suffice it to say, when you are learning how to maneuver a 39-foot sailboat into a tiny slip without crashing into wooden pilings or other boats, you are no longer thinking about playing coy for the camera. In fact, I was so preoccupied with the lessons that I completely forgot to bring the Go-Pro home with me after the class was over.

It was when I uploaded and watched my docking footage that I began to notice *me*. I had never really watched an extended video of myself before. I was able to see how I looked when I wasn't focused on how I looked. I saw how I laughed, how I smiled and how I interacted with other people.

And do you know what? I was so happy with what I saw. I thought it was beautiful. That might be strange to say about seeing yourself on TV, but I felt pride and love. I wanted to hug myself because I was so happy to see myself happy. I learned a lot more from that experience than how to properly dock a sailboat.

Now it's your turn. I'd like to challenge you to capture yourself unaware by creating your own self-montage. Let me give you a few suggestions to help you get started.

Set up a video camera in the family room during a busy weekend. See what happens as you begin to forget the camera is rolling. What face do you make when your child spills milk on the floor? Having a disagreement with your spouse? How does it look? How does it sound? Are you looking at your phone while your significant other is talking to you?

How about recruiting someone you trust to be your private paparazzi for a day or two? Once you have your special person selected, give them your camera and instruct them to take photos, or even better, extended video footage, as you go about your day or weekend. Their goal is for you to forget that they are there; this way you are less likely to "pose" for the camera, and the true you can be seen and captured.

What's the point of this challenge? Essentially, you want to see how others see you. But even more important, it's for you to really see yourself as you are, without any filters or editing. Feel free to go without makeup or keep that five-o'clock shadow. Relax, dress down and go as you are. Without being able to "fix" or "stage" the photos, you will get a more accurate representation of your true self.

We cannot expect to have happy faces on all the time, but the more aware we are of ourselves from all different viewpoints, the easier it will be to see how we might be able to change. As you become more content with the present moment, the happier you'll be. Now get out your camera and see what you can discover as you capture yourself unaware!

28

"Until one has loved an animal, a part of one's soul remains unawakened." —Anatole France

PEOPLE, PETS AND POSITIVITY

I talked earlier about the importance of surrounding yourself with a strong, positive support circle. However, it's not just the presence of people that can affect how you feel about your environment. Photographs, objects, words of wisdom and animals can also be a beneficial influence.

For example, you can choose to display lots of photos around your home or office. Select the moments that had a memorable impact on you, and make sure that *you* are included in most of the snapshots in order to remind you of your happy self. Remember to swap them out for newer ones on a regular basis so that they don't fade into the background and get overlooked.

You can also surround yourself with inspirational quotes and positive messages. Print them out and put them in decorative frames, select them as your computer's screen saver or your cell phone's wallpaper, or use them as your social media profile pictures or status updates. Sign up for a daily motivational text service. This can be an easy way to begin your day in the right mindset. If you choose to remain active on social media, select inspirational public figures or groups to follow and share with.

Do you have a pet? Do you want a pet? Animals are great companions and give endless amounts of unconditional love. Offer to pet-sit for a friend or, in a truly win-win scenario, sign up as a foster parent for sheltered or abandoned animals.

The key here is to create a space that fuels your desire to live your life with happiness, positive energy and a deep passion. In short, the more positive things you see, the more positive you feel.

29

"Kind words are short and easy to speak, but their echoes are truly endless." —Mother Teresa

FEED YOUR WOLF

Let me talk a little bit more about energy, or life energy, to be more specific.

A quick search on Google tells us a few things about life energy. It is the universal life force and every culture has its own name for this unique energy. In traditional Chinese culture, it's called *qi*; in Korean culture, it's *gi*; in Japanese culture, it's *ki*; and in Indian culture it's called *prana*, just to mention a few. It's the underlying principle behind the studies of such phenomena as chakras, auras and meridians of the human body.

Traditional Chinese medicine, yoga, meditation and many Asian martial arts are all examples of ways people can practice focusing and channeling their inner life force energy in order to bring about holistic healing, greater spiritual understanding, or even increased self-confidence and self-empowerment.

It is through Tae Kwon Do (TKD) that I learned my own life lesson about working to maintain a positive energy flow.

My children both train in TKD, so, as a family, we have

been a part of this special community for over four years now. With each new belt or level that is mastered, the students have to perform and demonstrate their knowledge to their teachers during a special ceremony. We have attended many of these belt assessments over the years, and, depending on how many students are participating at that time, these evaluations can last two hours or more.

One of the TKD Masters (the term "Master" is used to address a teacher as well as to show respect to elders) is famous for the "speeches" he gives at the conclusion of many of these belt ceremonies. Experienced and inspiring, he is from Korea and enjoys talking about everything from his personal experiences to the importance of fostering good character traits such as honor, respect and self-confidence. Just as you start to fidget in your seat, ready to go home, you'll hear something like, "Let me tell you a story." And everyone lets out a light-hearted sigh and smiles—we know we'll be there for at least another twenty minutes.

It was during one of these famous speeches, when I was just beginning to search for answers within my own journey, that I personally connected with one of his stories. Let me share with you my interpretation of the inspiring tale "Feed Your Wolf."

Picture in your mind, a wolf. Imagine we are talking about the gray wolf. The gray wolf is a beautiful, strong animal. By nature, they are social creatures and live in close-knit family packs. They can appear graceful and serene, yet at times they may also be fearsome and territorial.

Now, imagine that you have two of these gray wolves inside you. One is beautiful, strong and confident. The other is aggressive, loud and domineering. Each of these wolves is competing for its own survival, and they need a lot of food in order to survive.

How will you feed these two wolves? They don't eat the kind of food we eat, but rather it's the energy that we feel, create, absorb and project that gives them life. These energy vibrations can be positive, negative, strong or weak. As you may imagine, one wolf feeds on the positive energies, while the other feeds on the negative.

When we are feeling happy, strong, safe, powerful and confident, a lot of positive energy is created. This nourishes that beautiful, strong wolf inside us. Engaging in fun activities, hanging out with friends who make us laugh and feeling excited about life, create fuel for our positive wolf. As these positive and powerful energies become our aura, it will allow others to perceive us in a good way. People instinctively sense our confidence and joy, and feel safe and at ease around us.

By feeding this wolf, you will attract increasingly more positive things to you. Your mind will be more focused and clear, and your body will perform at its full potential while staying strong and vibrant. This is a healthy, happy you.

On the other hand, when we are feeling angry, defeated, resentful, sad or scared, negative energy is created, feeding that aggressive, domineering wolf. This wolf will force you to continue down the dark path of self-destruction. With this general aura of darker energy, people may perceive us in a more negative way. The more you feed this wolf, the more feelings of negativity and defeat will continue to overpower your life. Complaining, blaming others, feeding your own jealousy and not making the effort to enjoy the world and people around you are all sure ways to remain stuck in the rut of these negative energies.

By continuing to feed this wolf, you will start to feel trapped and cut off from pleasures that you may have once enjoyed. Your body will begin to shut down, making you feel lethargic and ill. Your mind will suffer, foggy with depressive thoughts and disappointments. This wolf brings out the defeated, unhealthy, you.

Why is this energy so important? Everything that you ever wanted to accomplish—to see, to do, to be—can be done by simply focusing on feeding the right wolf. It's truly dependent upon your state of mind. If you believe something is going to be difficult—it will be. If you feel confident that things will go well—they will. Even if they don't go as well as expected, you'll at least have an easier time working through it. With the right mindset and working to bring positive energy, greatness is possible.

Which wolf will you choose to feed today?

30

"The most dangerous risk of all: The risk of spending your life not doing what you want on the bet you can buy yourself the freedom to do it later." —Alan Watts

ONWARD WAVES

I am proud to say that *Onward Waves* is another amazing project, along with this book, that has evolved from my journey of self-discovery. This "senior project" of sorts has not only helped me stay focused on keeping my inner spark alight but has also become a way for my children, my husband and myself to spend quality time together. Let me tell you more about this sailing adventure story that we call *Onward Waves*.

When my tumultuous road to self-discovery began, both my husband and I were challenged beyond belief. We were forced to face obstacles that neither one of us ever anticipated, and yet we consider ourselves lucky, because we have persevered and have so far survived our hurdles. Not everyone can say the same. It certainly wasn't easy, and it most certainly wasn't much fun, but through it all, we have grown closer and more united in both our marriage and as a family unit than we had ever been before.

A lot of puzzle pieces coming together is what truly led to

this unique and transformational change in our life story. Remember the Ted Talk I listened to about the pursuit of a memorable life? Remember when I moved out of my house and when my husband became ill? Remember when I began questioning what was really important to me? And do you also remember when I encouraged trying new things and to face your fears? All of these pieces of my story contributed to how we got from what seemed like certain divorce to our newfound love, respect, and a desire to truly enjoy our lives together.

The idea of buying a boat and sailing off into the sunset started out innocently enough. My husband and I were simply searching for a change—a change that would bring us and our family closer together. It was during that search, that a sailboat caught my husband's eye. Then he showed it to me. And then he showed me another one, and another one. We began to imagine—the four of us, on a boat, in the ocean. Could we?

After the intense strains on our marriage, it was easy to indulge in daydreaming about "living on island time" with less stress, endless tranquil blue waters, piña coladas and sunsets galore. We joked with each other about who would be the "captain" and who would be the "first mate." We even thought that the close proximity of living on a boat might actually be just what we needed.

Then we started looking at more sailboats online. Specifically, the ones that were for sale. The stresses seemed to fade away with every new boat listing we clicked on. We investigated even more by reading blogs and watching videos of other families living and sailing the world together. We saw that a sailing lifestyle could also offer us another thing that we craved, more time with our children, to watch them grow and help them discover all the beauty and true diversity the world has to offer.

Soon, our joking turned more serious. I remember saying to my husband, "I don't want to keep talking and fantasizing about living on a sailboat. If we really want to do this, let's figure out a way to make it happen." And from that moment, we plunged headfirst into making this adventure a reality.

What does this adventure really mean for us? It means that we are actively planning to sell our house, buy a sailboat, move aboard and embark on a one- to two-year family sailing adventure. While we would love to cast off the lines today, we don't want to be too haphazard or irresponsible. We want to do it right. So that means good planning, organization and a lot of learning.

We began researching what the lifestyle of a liveaboard family really entailed, including things like finances and other logistics. We wanted to educate ourselves even more, so we enrolled in sailing courses and bought lots of books—books on everything from sailing techniques and fundamentals, to marine diesel engine maintenance and repair. Then we joined a local sailing club to get more hands-on sailing experience. Currently, we attend sailboat shows whenever we can and we are saving money and pinching pennies in every way possible. We (our kids included) are constantly brainstorming to discover unique ways to help us reach our goal sooner!

When we first began pitching our sailing idea to our children they were both pretty excited. Even today, as we're getting closer to making it a reality, they are completely on board (pun intended!) with the idea of living and exploring life while on a sailboat. By now, they are used to talking about boats, they know the sailing lingo and they are aware of the changes that this adventure will bring to our lives, like having school taught by mom and dad! Their biggest concerns are when it comes to the idea of selling our house. Understandably, they have strong emotional attachments to it since it's the only home they have ever known. Their other concerns are about missing their friends and wondering if they will be held back a grade when we return from our trip. We have eased their worries by letting them know that we will do our absolute best when it comes to boat-schooling and keeping them caught up with all their study requirements. We will also have an "open-boat" policy where friends and family are always welcome to visit. In short, our children know that they have a voice that will be heard during this whole process.

As this transformation started growing and taking shape, and telling family and friends about our plan became imminent, my husband and I searched for a way to really bring our dream to life. We wanted to show them just how serious we were. So, we branded our transformation by giving it a memorable name, an appealing logo and a catchy tagline! Our abstract butterfly design reads: *Onward Waves—Even the smallest ripple can change the world.*

We were a little hesitant to tell our friends and family about our plan at first; when you don't even have a sailboat or a definitive departure date, it can make it seem more like a fantasy than a reality. But once we began sharing our story, and they could see how serious we were, they, too, were on board, freely voicing any questions and concerns—whether about safety issues or schooling for the kids. So far, we have been met with nothing but positive support and a whole bunch of people rooting for us and our story. Not only that, but several people have told us that our uplifting story has inspired them to begin making positive changes in their own lives.

We crafted this dream because we believe in each other and because we believe in others. Our mission is to actively pursue moments that will stay with us year after year while encouraging kindness and joy to spread like wildfire. If we can help bring about positive change to even just one person's life, we will truly feel blessed. And if we can inspire others to make changes in order to truly love the life they live, then that is *Onward Waves*.

As I note on our website, life seems to pass in the blink of an eye. We are often left wondering where the time has gone. *Onward Waves* is an idea that was born from our desires to live a more simple, happy, and more fulfilled life while inspiring others to do the same. We chose to use a butterfly image to symbolize the "butterfly effect" idea that goes along with the founding principles of the scientific chaos theory. This theory suggests that with even the smallest of occurrence, such as the flap of a butterfly's wing, there is a potential to create enormous change.

We want the name *Onward Waves* and our butterfly image to be synonymous with the concept of loving the life you live and consciously working towards that. This doesn't mean you need lots of expensive, foreign or extravagant things in order to do that—or that you have to completely turn your life upside-down like us. It simply means that by just doing things that bring you joy and contentment, you not only open the possibility of welcoming more positive change to your life, but you also positively impact the lives of other people as well. We believe that by consciously creating memorable moments each day we can all live a life worth remembering.

I invite you to visit our webpage at www.OnwardWaves.com to read more about our story. You can also follow along on our adventure as we post videos and pictures on our blog, Facebook, and Instagram.

Will we inspire you?

31

"When you do the common things in life in an uncommon way, you will command the attention of the world." —George Washington Carver

THE SAME OLD, SAME OLD: TAKE II

This book wouldn't feel complete if I didn't mention some of the other, more common ways of increasing happiness in your life. You have probably heard many of these before and, like me, may have rolled your eyes a little each time they passed through your ears. The eye-rolling doesn't come from a place of ill will, but rather from being tired of hearing the same old tune while feeling that there just has to be something more.

Once I started feeling happier within myself, some of these more common ideas began to take on new meaning. Let me take a moment to mention a few of these ideas here, because they may help you on your journey, too, when you're ready for them.

- **Donate** old clothes, toys, food, furniture and vehicles. You will feel good knowing someone else will have less burden and stress in their life just because you did a little spring cleaning.

- **Volunteer** your time. Create memories and spread kindness. Then share your story with us at *Onward Waves*.

- Use your **gift of gab**. Talk to strangers. You'll learn a lot about others, but also a lot about yourself. Not to mention fact that you can make someone's day just by saying, "Hello! How are you today?"

- Get enough **shut-eye**. A good night's sleep is important. If you feel like you are not regularly getting a restful sleep, I urge you to investigate. Figure out what may be causing the interruption. Things like stress, teeth grinding or sleep apnea can not only interrupt your sleep cycle, they can be signs of more serious health issues.

- **Natural remedies**. There is a pill out there for every problem, condition and disease. There are even pills for the side effects of the pills that you take. Don't be so quick to rely on a prescription drug to solve your problems. First, do a little investigating. Try looking into your diet, for example, and how your body processes the foods you're consuming. Adding simple spices such as curcumin (an ingredient found in turmeric), Ceylon cinnamon, and fenugreek (found in Indian cuisines) have been shown to have similar therapeutic effects as many of the chemical drugs that are being prescribed. Healthier alternatives

are out there, and it's up to you to be the advocate
for your health. Having a doctor that you trust is
also important, as it will allow you the comfort to
ask more questions. Resort to prescription
medication only when absolutely necessary.

- **Stay healthy**. Keep up with your whole-body
  preventative care appointments and follow
  through with the recommended treatment
  measures. Preventative care should include regular
  visits to your dentist and primary care physician.
  Other preventative measures you can explore
  include things like chiropractic, acupuncture,
  meditation, prayer and yoga.

- **Yum Yum Yum**. Remember, you are what you
  eat. Consume everything in moderation. Try to use
  food as fuel rather than as a crutch. Be mindful of
  any allergies or sensitivities that you may have.
  There are also lots of health benefits to fasting.
  Whole body cleansing of sugars and carbohydrates
  can provide a jumpstart to your energy levels.
  However, always speak with your doctor first
  before beginning any new diet or major health
  change.

- **Limit alcohol** and other mood modifiers.
  Things like alcohol and certain drugs, like
  marijuana, have an overall depressant effect on
  your state of mind. They work by disrupting the
  chemical balance in our brains. While it may feel
  good initially to have your inhibitions loosen and
  your worries seem to disappear, too much of these

can lead to more serious negative effects. If you are having feelings of sadness or other negative emotions on a regular basis, the last thing you want is additional depressants working against you. Subduing or otherwise trying to escape from your emotions will not help you heal. Staying as chemical-free as you can will always be favored. Your mind and body work their best when you have both mental and emotional clarity.

- You gotta **work out**. Yes, I have to mention it, because exercise may be more important than you think. An article published in *Comprehensive Physiology* suggests that physical inactivity is a primary cause of most chronic diseases—such as heart disease, cancer and diabetes. That's a big deal. So, don't wait. Make it a point to add some heart-pumping movement to your life, starting today.

- Find a side **passion**. Finding even a small hobby that brings enjoyment into your life works wonders on a sad soul. Start a fire in your belly by remembering the little things that used to bring you joy as a child. Get out those crayons, paper and scissors—or try something new. Just put yourself out there to experience the many things this world has to offer.

- Spend some time **grounding** yourself. Go outdoors and enjoy nature. Take your shoes off and connect with the earth, one on one. Grounding is said to help by working with the positive and negative electrons within our bodies and of the earth itself. Remember the importance of having good energy? I know a certain wolf that might like this idea. If you can't squeeze in some barefoot-in-the-park time, you can buy an earthing mat to sleep on at night.

- Develop a **spiritual practice**.
Religion/Spirituality can be a touchy subject, but finding something that guides you and makes you feel more complete is always going to be a welcome change. There may be only one true universal truth, but there are many ways to learn about it, experience it and celebrate it. Choose the path that means the most to you.
- Be **courageous** and **believe** in yourself. No one else can make you happy. Only you have the power to do that. Once you believe in this, that subtle glow coming from within your core will begin to burn brighter and brighter.

Allow these "same old, same old" tips to help you as you start welcoming more change, challenge, and inspiration into your life. Hopefully, they'll offer something new and rewarding on your journey toward the truly happy you.

You are meant for joy. You are meant to survive. You are meant to thrive. I believe in you.

32

"People are like stained-glass windows. They sparkle and shine when the sun is out, but when the darkness sets in, their true beauty is revealed only if there is a light from within." —Elisabeth Kubler-Ross

PACKING UP AND CALLING IT A DAY

My sincere hope is that some of my experiences have left a positive and encouraging impression. I hope that by sharing my stories and thoughts, someone, somewhere will feel inspired. And maybe someone, somewhere will start making changes in their life. And someone, somewhere will have smiled a little more, laughed out loud, found a spark inside their belly, and grown confident that they, too, can be brave enough to love themselves and this life they live. And maybe that someone is you.

The hardest part of any self-transformation is accepting that you need it. Many people say they want change. But those of us who have accepted that we actually *need* the change will be the ones to persevere. The next challenge is finding the remedy that works for you. Hopefully, some of the concepts and exercises I have provided here will give you a good foundation to start. Deciding which first step to take is up to you. No matter what you choose, know that it is a good first step because you chose it.

Consciously working to create memorable moments is not always easy. However, when you commit your mind to this goal, you will find that a transformation can occur at any time.

As we say with *Onward Waves*—even the smallest ripple can change the world. If just a small act of love, kindness, thoughtfulness, courage or understanding is enough to change the world, imagine what it can do just for your whole self. You'll be living a more joyful, fulfilled, and passionate life before you know it.

33

"There is no path to happiness. Happiness is the path." —Gautama Buddha

LET'S REVIEW

I have shared quite a bit with you here. I have shared some of my most challenging experiences as well as my most significant moments of personal growth. All of these things have helped me rediscover my true joy. I finally sense the spark burning deep in my core. I have found true purpose in my life. Hopefully, I have been able to provide a guide for you to do the same.

Let's do a quick review of the chapters and their key concepts. Which ones will help you discover your truly happy self? Try them and find out.

1. Pursue the things you are passionate about. Make a list of your interests and skills to help guide you to that passion.
2. Allow yourself to trust and feel empowered by your decisions and choices.
3. Release those heavy anchors that keep you stuck in

the past. Ask yourself, "How long ago did most of these things that I am holding on to take place?"

4. Fully engage your five senses. Experience the beauty of the world that surrounds you each day.

5. Enjoy this moment right now. Work on practicing mindfulness throughout each day.

6. Quiet your ego's negative chatter and work to make it a more positive narrator. Reward yourself with some alone time every now and then. Maybe you can use that time to participate in those newfound passions that you've discovered.

7. Be open and ready for an "ah-ha" moment. Let it teach and propel you forward during your journey.

8. Work on becoming more minimalistic. You'll appreciate the things that you currently have a whole lot more.

9. Break out of your shell and try something new. Sailing? Painting? Soap making?

10. Don't let your fears consume you or hold you back from living your life. Acknowledge them and keep pushing forward.

11. Who is the most important person right now? You are. Don't forget that.

12. Look who's laughing now! What are some things that get you to laugh, smile or let out a snicker? Keep up a positive attitude and laugh your cares away.

13. Surround yourself with a loving, supportive and uplifting team—and be the same to others who are in your life.

14. Instead of cluttering your mind with drama from

the past, choose to fill it with the special little moments. Work towards creating more of these little moments each day.

15. Be a good friend. Give good hugs and get together, in person.

16. Use your voice and feel confident in yourself. Don't let unstated expectations become barriers between you and a more joyful life.

17. Wisdom can be gained in unexpected places. Whether you prepare your runway for takeoff or get a paintbrush ready, find easy techniques to help clear your mind. Be open to learning lessons. A more peaceful and calm you is just ahead.

18. Deadlines? Who needs 'em?!

19. Rewind and rediscover your childhood drive. This is your life. Choose to believe in your abilities to make it great.

20. Love yourself. All of it. Inside and out. Be grateful for everything you've already done in life and everything that is to come.

21. Take your own good advice.

22. Give social media a rest every now and then.

23. Capture yourself unaware. Who are you when you think no one's looking?

24. Surround yourself with positive people, photos, objects or inspirational quotes. Consider the unconditional love of a pet.

25. Choose your wolf and feed him or her well.

26. *Onward Waves*—even the smallest ripple can change the world. Are you loving the life you live?

I hope that by telling my stories and showing you that it is possible to face the demons inside, break through, and reawaken your true self, you'll find the determination to do the same.

Welcome to the truly happy you.

Additional Information

Here are some of the resources that I mentioned within the book, used as a reference, or that have generally influenced me during my journey.

Books:

Eckhart Tolle is a fabulous writer and speaker. He has also had a remarkable journey to self-discovery. I highly recommend his books or at least doing a quick search of his quotes; they speak volumes, yet are so simple. Let them speak to you as they did for me.

Some recommended readings are:

- *Many Lives, Many Masters* by Brian L. Weiss, M.D.
- *The Untethered Soul: The Journey Beyond Yourself* by Michael A. Singer
- *Eat, Pray, Love* by Elizabeth Gilbert
- *A New Earth: Awakening Your Life's Purpose* by Eckhart Tolle
- *The Power of Now: A Guide to Spiritual Enlightenment* by Eckhart Tolle

Seminars, Retreats, and New-Age or Holistic Therapies:

Regarding the concept of mindfulness, there are many books and articles you can read to learn more. The book that got me started was, again, Eckhart Tolle's *The Power of Now*. There are also many seminars and lectures on mindfulness, such as the one I attended at Yogaville. The following business descriptions are taken directly from the individual websites.

- Satchidananda Ashram Yogaville in Buckingham, Buckingham, VA. "Retreat from the modern world and reconnect to your best self. Our expert presenters lead you in explorations of health, spiritual inquiry, joy, and creativity." Yogaville offers meditation sessions, yoga classes, prayer center as well as comfortable accommodations, healthy vegetarian meals and beautiful surroundings. Visit the website at www.yogaville.org.

- The Esalen Institute in Big Sur, California. Esalen, a nonprofit organization, "is an alternative educational center devoted to the exploration of the human potential and personal and social transformation. Situated on 27 acres of spectacular Big Sur coastline, Esalen offers over 550 workshops, bodywork, an intensive work-study program and other enrichment activities." Visit their website at www.esalen.org.

- Kelly Lynn Gitter, Therapist. Creator and founder of 8Choices. Kelly has created "a personal and business consulting firm that is powered by the belief that reality exists because of us, not in spite of us. Utilizing evolved business practices and innovative theory, they are committed to transformation through the expansion of consciousness. Kelly and her team are dedicated to fostering an environment that supports the development of healthy, happy and authentic individuals and organizations..." Visit her website at www.8choices.com.

- Courtney D. Starkey, M.Ed., CHt, Hypnosis. Courtney is a hypnotist and a children's book author who has trained with many leaders in the field of hypnosis, including Dr. Brian Weiss, author of *Many Lives, Many Masters.* "Hypnosis is a truly amazing resource for understanding and healing many of life's issues and it has tremendous potential to help one heal and grow..." mentally, emotionally and spiritually. Visit her website at www.payitforwardhypnosis.com.

Educational Resources, Articles, and Studies:

- *Laughter: A Scientific Investigation* by Robert Provine, PhD, a psychologist at the University of Maryland-Baltimore County. (www.provine.umbc.edu/books/laughter-a-scientific-investigation)
- *The Effect of Humor on Short-Term Memory in Older Adults: a new component for whole-person wellness.* (www.ncbi.nlm.nih.gov/pubmed/24682001)
- *Give Your Body a Boost—With Laughter* (www.webmd.com/balance/features/give-your-body-boost-with-laughter)
- *Does Hugging Provide Stress-Buffering Social Support? A study of susceptibility to upper*

respiratory infection and illness
(www.psy.cmu.edu/~scohen/Does%20Hugging.pdf)

- *Why We Need at Least 8 Hugs a Day* published on
  Mind Body Green. (www.mindbodygreen.com/o-
  5756/10-Reasons-Why-We-Need-at-Least-8-
  Hugs-a-Day)
- *"The Science of Happiness–New Discoveries for a
  More Joyful Life"*, *TIME* magazine, 2016.
- *Lack of Exercise Is a Major Cause of Chronic
  Diseases* by Frank W. Booth, Christian K. Roberts,
  Matthew J. Laye. Comprehensive Physiology
  2012, 2: 1143-1211. doi: 10.1002/cphy.c110025

Other Helpful Websites:

- TED Talks "are influential videos from expert
  speakers on education, business, science, tech and
  creativity that are offered in over 100 languages."
  You can find thousands of inspirational,
  informative and powerful short video talk sessions
  at www.ted.com.
- The online social networking portal Meetup.com
  facilitates offline group meetings. This allows
  members to find and join groups unified by a
  common interest, such as politics, books, games,
  movies, health, pets, careers or hobbies.

Review Request

Did you enjoy reading *The Truly Happy You: A Simple Guide to Reigniting Your Inner Spark?* Please let me know your thoughts by leaving a book review. Your feedback not only helps me, it helps others who may be on a similar quest for joy to find their way here.

Spread the Word

Do you know someone that might need to read *The Truly Happy You: A Simple Guide to Reigniting Your Inner Spark?* Feel free to share and spread the word on social media and use the hashtag #OnwardWaves.

Contact Me

I'd love to hear from you! Find me on:

Twitter (@HearOutLoudBlog)
Facebook (www.facebook.com/onwardwaves)
Online at (www.OnwardWaves.com)

Please feel free to check in and follow up on where I am in my journey, tell me something about your own, or tell me how *The Truly Happy You* has helped reignite *your* inner spark.

ABOUT THE AUTHOR

Jessica (Abele) Briceno grew up in Lancaster, Pennsylvania. After receiving her B.S in Communications from the Indiana University of Pennsylvania in August of 2000, she moved to Houston,Texas to try her hand at magazine editing and publication. Jessica later went on to complete a second degree to become a registered dental hygienist from the Massachusetts College of Pharmacy and Health Sciences.

After her own intense journey to self-discovery, Jessica felt a strong desire to help others who were struggling with things like self-acceptance, self-worth or those simply searching for a greater sense of inner peace and happiness. Jessica wrote *The Truly Happy You* as a way to tell her personal stories, share lessons learned and, most importantly, to offer unique guidance. By reading and working through this book, Jessica hopes to help the reader learn how to smile a little wider, laugh a little louder and realize that they, too, have a spark glowing within.

Jessica currently lives in the D.C. area with her husband and her two children.

For more information:

www.OnwardWaves.com
TheTrulyHappyYou@gmail.com

ACKNOWLEDGMENTS

I am writing my acknowledgements page, which means I am finally finished with my book. What a journey! There are so many people that I need to thank; this book draws on stories from my entire life, and there have been so many people—memorable, influential, and wonderful people—along for this ride. Honestly, my journey, and this book, would not have been the same without them.

First and foremost, I want to thank my husband, Diego. *Mi amor*, thank you for being you and thank you for loving me. I hope that with the truly happier me, the Jess 2.0, we can continue creating memorable moments together. TQM!

To my children, Nicolas and Caprice: I am so proud of both of you. I hope that you will continue to grow up knowing just how important, unique, and loved you are. I am so blessed to have you in my life. You teach me new things all the time, and above all, you inspire me to be the best Mommy that I can be. You have the whole world to explore, and your spark will help guide your way! I can't wait to see what you can do!

I am very thankful for my immediate family—my mom, my dad and Linda, Megan, and Dan. To my grandparents, aunts, uncles, and cousins—thank you, too. I hope that we will always work to make our relationship great.

My extended family also includes many wonderful people —I am among the lucky ones who have been blessed with amazing in-laws! Much love and gratitude to the Carbrica family for your continued love and support, including Sylvia, Luis, Adriana, and Julian, and the Dallas branch: Diana, Gustavo, Arturo, Guillermo, and Santiago. Much love to Eduardo ("Ado") and Margaret, and also the one and only Maria (aka "Potota"). And to my soul couple, Sam and Christel Saab, whom I consider honorary family, thank you. You are such great cheerleaders to have in my corner—let's keep this party going! And I can't forget giving a special shout-out to all of my "inherited" Venezuelan brothers, sisters, and friends.

As I said, there have been so many people who have played a significant role in my life, whether in the past or with each new day. I want to thank you for giving me what I needed to make my story even more memorable. If you are reading this far, and you see your name listed here, I hope it brings as large a smile to your face as it did mine. Please know that I have a special place in my heart for you, and, even if we never cross paths again, I feel blessed beyond belief for the time we have shared.

J.P. McCaskey High School rules! A huge shout-out to Ganga, Jason, Karl, Patrick, John M., Joe, Matt, Phil, Jen V.B., Krista, Christelle, Rob, Heather K., Krystal, Susan, Jamael, Carrie, Chrissy (and all my fellow band geeks), Alisan, Hao, Kim, Jedd, Andy, Aeriel, Mike, Lennel, Jackie, Heather R.,

Rod, Angel, Omar, Corinne, and Nisa (and all my basketball buddies).

To my IUP crowd. We sure have some crazy stories logged, don't we? Cheers to Lisa, Lyndi, Amber, Jen, Julie, Brian, Kevin, Bill, Laura, Jodi, and my TPA sisters.

I'd like to recognize a few more special people who have entered my life within the past eleven years. I am so happy that we have shared time together and I thank you for your friendship. Jen and Mike M., Rafael and Lupita, Ligia and Marcos, Brian and Mary Karen (MK, you got me thinking about writing a book in the first place and are an inspiration to many, myself included—thank you for sharing your spark with me.) Also to Donna, Lori, and Grandmaster Seung-min Choi and Majest Martial Arts. Some wonderful dentists who I have had the pleasure to work with and learn from are: Dr. Rick Jackomis, Dr. Sandhya Pal, Dr. Gopal Pal, Dr. Radwa Sobeih, Dr. Fadi Alhrashi, and Dr.Minh-an La-Pham. I also want to thank the many amazing patients who I have had the opportunity to meet and care for over the years. And to Kelly and all my journey friends—thank you for being a part of my spiritual awakening.

And finally, a ginormous thank you to all the people who helped me turn my book into a book! To my fantastic editor, Andrea Robinson, and her red bubbles of inspiration: I'll be forever grateful. Thank you to Gustavo Villareal for your creative intuition that led to my amazing cover design, and to Jay Fondin for taking that design and making it work. And a gracious thank you to Jessica Snyder for a quick and thorough proofread. And thank you to the writer friends from my Meetup group, especially Gail Herndon for being my first "reader" and C.J. Ellisson for helping me get my book off my computer and into the hands of others!

92823767R00145

Made in the USA
Columbia, SC
03 April 2018